The Selected Works of Gabriel Deville
First Prism Key Press Edition 2011

Prism Key Press
New York, NY 10001
PrismKeyPress.com

ISBN-13: 978-1468081527

The Selected Works of Gabriel Deville

CONTENTS

The Materialistic Conception of History

By study, and by observation of the phenomena of inorganic and organic Nature, Man becomes conscious of their relations of cause and effect and becomes more and more the master of his own development.

Before co-ordinating his ideas and grasping their different relations, man acts. This is true, both in the childhood of the individual and the race. But it is only from the time that it becomes subordinate to deliberate thought that his action ceases to be incoherent and becomes really and rapidly effective. And what is true of every other kind of action is true of revolutionary action. It must have science for its guide, or its puerile efforts will produce only abortive effects.

No matter what the subject may be, to maintain that science is useless or that study has had its day, is only an idle pretext to avoid study or an attempt to excuse wilful, persistent ignorance.

It is evident that the study of social life, alone and of itself, will not modify the social form and will not furnish, elaborated in the smallest details, the ground-plan and elevation of a new society; but it will disclose the constituent elements of the present society; their essential combinations and relations, their tendencies and the law which prevails over their evolution. This knowledge will put us in a position, not "to abolish by decrees the natural phases of the development of modern society, but to shorten the period of pregnancy and to mitigate the pangs of child-birth."

By preaching the thorough study of society, Karl Marx did not pretend to be the creator of a science unknown before him. This is proven by the numerous notes to his work, which is on the contrary, based on the labor of the economists who preceded him, and he had the courage and candor, in the case of every proposition, to cite the author who first formulated it. But no one has done more than Karl Marx to make plain by their analysis the true meaning and tendency of social phenomena. No one, therefore, has done more for the emancipation of the working-class, for the emancipation of humanity.

Yes, without doubt, others, before him, felt the social injustices and grew righteously indignant. Many were those who dreamt of remedying these evils and drew up on paper admirable projects of reform. Inspired by a laudable generosity, having in most cases a very clear perception of the sufferings of the masses, they criticized with as much justice as eloquence the existing order of things. But as they had no exact conception of its causes and its evolution they constructed (on paper) model societies that were none the less chimerical because their architects had some correct intuitions. If they had the universal welfare as a motive, they did no have reality as a guide.

In their projects of social renovation, they entirely disregarded facts, pretending to have recourse only to the pure light of reason, as if reason, which is only the co-ordination and generalization of the ideas furnished by experience, could be, in itself, a source of knowledge – knowledge external and superior to the cerebral modifications of external impressions.

In a word, they were idealists, just as the anarchists are today. Instead of making reality the starting point of their reasoning, they attribute reality to the fictions born of their particular ideal of absolute justice.

Finding, from the speculative point of view, that the most agreeable of all social regimes would be that which would permit the most unrestricted freedom to the blossoming of individuality, and which would have no law save the free will of individuals, the anarchists preach its realization without troubling themselves to enquire whether the economic necessities permit of its establishment. They do not suspect the retrograde character of the extreme individualism, the unlimited autonomy, which is the essence of anarchism.

In the various orders of facts, evolution is invariably accomplished by the transition from an incoherent form, from a state of diffusion to a state of concentration. And, as the concentration of the parts becomes greater, their reciprocal interdependence increases, that is to say, that more and more they cannot extend the range of their own activity without the co-operation of the other parts. This is a general truth that the anarchists do not suspect. Poor fellows! They pretend to see further than anyone else, but they do not perceive that they are marching backwards.

For all these fanciful conceptions – although more or less well meant – Marx was the first to substitute the study of social phenomena based on the real conception – the materialist conception. He did not sing the praises of a system more or less perfect from the subjective point of view. He scrupulously examined the facts, methodically arranged the results of his examination and drew the conclusion, which was and is the scientific explanation of the historical progress of humanity, and particularly, of the capitalist period through which we are passing.

History, he has shown, is nothing but the history of class conflicts. The division of society into classes, which made its appearance with the same social life of man, rests on economic relations – maintained by force – which enable some to succeed in shifting on to the shoulders of others the natural necessity to labor.

Material interests have always been the inciting motives of the incessant struggles of the privileged classes, either with each other, or against the inferior classes at whose expense they live. Man is dominated by the material conditions of life, and these conditions, and therefore the mode of production, have determined and will determine human customs, ethics and institutions – social, economic, political, juridical, etc.

As soon as one part of society has monopolized the means of production, the other part, upon whom the burden of labor falls, is obliged to add to the labor-time necessary for its own support, a certain surplus labor time, for which it receives no equivalent, – time that is devoted to supporting and enriching the possessors of the means of production. As an extractor of unpaid labor, which, by means of the increasing surplus-value whose source it is, accumulates every day, more and more, in the hands of the proprietary class the instruments of its domination, the capitalist regime surpasses in power all the antecedent regimes founded on compulsory labor.

But, today, the economic conditions begotten by this regime, trammelled in their natural evolution by this very regime, inexorably tend to break the capitalist mold which can no longer contain them, and these destroying principles are the elements of the new society.

The historic mission of the class at present exploited – the proletariat – which is being organized and disciplined by the very mechanism of production, is to complete the work of destruction begun by the development of social antagonisms. It must, first of all, definitely wrest from its class adversaries the political power – the command of the force devoted by them to preserving intact their economic monopolies and privileges.

Once in control of the political power, it will be able, by proceeding to the socialization of the means of production through the expropriation of the usurpers of the fruits of others toil, to suppress the present contradictions between collective production and private capitalist appropriation, and to realize the universalization of labor and the abolition of classes.

Such is a summary sketch of the irrefutable theory taught by Marx. His constant aim is to enable every reader to judge its truth and validity for himself.

As thought is nothing but the intellectual reflex of the real movement of things, he has not for an instant departed from the material foundation of his thought, from external phenomena; he has not separated man from the conditions of his existence. He has observed, he has stated the result of his observation, and purely by the depth of his analysis he has complemented his positive conception of the present order by the knowledge of the inevitable dissolution of this order.

Socialism, Revolution and Internationalism

I

Socialism, revolution, internationalism—these are the three subjects regarding which I beg your permission to say what—with no pretence of being infallible—I believe to be the truth. At the risk of telling you nothing new, I will simply try to speak truth. Those who reproach the socialists for constantly repeating the same thing, have, no doubt, the habit of accommodating the truth to suit their taste for variety. On the other hand, to talk of socialism is to do what everyone else is doing at this time, but I will speak to you of it from the standpoint of a socialist, and—unhappily—that is not as yet equally common.

The signal and distinctive mark of modern socialism is that it springs directly from the facts. Far from resting on the imaginary conceptions of the intellect, from being a more or less utopian vision of an ideal society, socialism is to-day simply the theoretical expression of the contemporaneous phase of the economic evolution of humanity.

At this point we are met with two objections.

On the one hand, because we say that socialism springs from the facts, we are accused of denying the influence of the Idea and the liberal defenders of the Idea rise up in revolt; they can calm themselves again. How could we deny the influence of the Idea, when socialism itself is as yet, as I have just pointed out, only a theoretical expression, *i.e.*, an idea, which we nevertheless believe has a certain influence?

We merely assert that a truth, irrevocably established by science as a valid generalization, does not cease to be a truth when it is applied to human history and socialism. This truth is the action of the environment: all living beings are the product of the environment in which they live. To the environment, in the last analysis, to the relations necessarily created by the multiple contacts, actions and reactions of the environment and the environed are due all the transformations of all organisms and, in consequence, all the phenomena that emanate from them. Thought is one of these phenomena, and, just like all the others, it has its source in actual facts. To say that socialism springs from the facts, is then simply to place the socialist idea on the same plane with all other ideas. In socialism, as in all subjects, the idea is the reflex in the brain of the relations of man with his surroundings, and the greater or less aptitude of the brain for acquiring, retaining and combining ideas, constitutes intelligence. The latter, in making various combinations out of the elements provided by the environment, may obviously lose sight of the reality which serves as its foundation, but our socialism aims never to depart from the data drawn from unbiased observation of the facts.

We are accused, on the other hand, because we believe that the economic question contains the whole of socialism, of denying the existence and influence of the intellectual factor, the sentimental factor, the psychological factor—in short, a whole collection of factors. Now, as I am going to try to show you, our only error, if it is an error, is that we wish to put the cart behind the horse, and to accuse us of wishing to suppress the cart because we refuse to put it in front or alongside of the horse, proves, at once, the incontestable desire to find us at fault, and the difficulty of gratifying that desire.

Man, as I said just now, is the product of the environment. But, to the influence of the cosmic or natural environment, which affects all beings, there was soon joined in his case the influence of the special environment created by him, an environment resulting from the acquired means of action, from the material of the tools used, from the conditions of life added by him to those furnished him by nature, or else substituted for them, the influence, in a word, of the economic environment, an influence which has gradually become predominant because the conditions of life, determining in all orders of society man's mode of life, have finally become less and less dependent upon the purely physical capabilities of the cosmic environment, and more and more dependent upon the means of action acquired by human exertions, upon the artificial capabilities of the economic environment, upon human thought materialized in various innovations.

We find at the foundation of everything affecting man the influence of the natural and economic environments, and, if it is quite true that we recognize the preponderant influence of the economic environment, it is passing strange to accuse us of not recognizing the action of human intelligence, which we assert is the creator of this environment. Only we do not forget that, at any stage of development whatever, intelligence does nothing by its creations except to elaborate the elements which it finds "ready made," as it were, in the environment.

Therefore, intelligence can, by working with the elements furnished by the existing environment, produce a change in this environment. This new environment thus changed becomes the determining environment of future intelligence. You see that, far from degrading the role of intelligence, we attribute to it a considerable importance; we only refuse to see in it a spontaneous phenomenon.

Having replied to the reproach of not taking into consideration what is called intelligence and is paraded as the intellectual factor, it is scarcely necessary for me to honor with special replies all the other factors mobilized against us, as they are all merely products of intelligence. I will remark, however, that if it is true that we do not deduce our theory from this association of factors, this does not authorize the conclusion that morality, right, justice, psychology, and sentiment are for us words devoid of meaning. To refuse to elevate them to the rank of scientific proofs, which is what we do, and all that we do, is not to deny them; it is simply to avoid employing them for a use for which they are not and could not be destined. Because, to uphold our theory, we prefer to have recourse to the observation of facts and their tendencies, we have never proscribed the

15

conception or sentiment of justice as motives for adhesion to that very theory, and we do not hesitate to declare that that which is unfitted to serve as a scientific proof, may be utilized as a motive for action.

Moreover, even those who attribute to the "syndicate" of factors a preponderating power over historical progress do not attribute to intelligence a greater influence than we recognize as belonging to it. In fact, the controversy here is not concerning the influence of ideas. The controversy arises when we attempt to determine which ideas are influential. On either side it is simply a matter of choosing from among the products of intelligence. Our opponents insist upon the claims of the factors in combination, instead of recognizing, as do we, the predominant influence of the ideas which clothe themselves in the phenomenal form of acts, such as inventions, etc., which lead to the modification of the economic environment and consequently, as we believe, to the modification of man himself, in his mode of life first, in his habits and methods of thought afterward.

As soon as it is seen that the transformation of the economic conditions, of the conditions of life, is the fundamental transformation, that upon which all the others are more or less dependent, it will be recognized that to say that socialism is simply the expression of the contemporaneous phase of economic conditions is not to narrow, in the slightest degree, its field of action, but only to define more accurately its immediate goal. The affirmation that there is in progress an evolution of the economic environment implies necessarily a corresponding evolution of the various branches of human knowledge, which are all influenced by this environment, just as the apple-tree implies the apple without its being necessary to speak of the integral apple-tree.[1] If socialism is contained "in a purely economic formula," it is just as the apple-tree is contained in the seed. Let us be vigilant to see that this "economic formula" and this seed are not thwarted in their normal development, and we shall have all the fruits that may

16

be desired, even if we refrain from heaping qualifying or complemental adjectives upon the apple-tree and socialism.

Some have thought that they have discovered an argument against this predominance of the economic environment and of the economic question, in the fact that some events which are not economic in nature—and revocation of the edict of Nantes—have had a great influence on human history. They forget that, if such or such an important event was not directly in itself an economic phenomenon, it is chiefly by the consequences that it had from the economic point of view that it became important; like all human discoveries, all historic events, it reached a point where it became a modifying element of the economic environment.

To recapitulate, if we insist upon the influence of the surroundings, and, particularly, upon the preponderant influence of the economic environment—the creation of man—this does not justify representing us as attributing an exclusive influence to the economic environment and as holding that this environment itself is created and influenced only by facts properly classed as economic.

I return then to my first proposition: socialism must have and has for its foundation the economic environment, the economic facts. What are those facts?

II

In order for man, who can live only on condition that he works, to be able to perform any sort of work, he must have at his disposition the instruments and the subject of labor. Now, these tools and this material, in one word, the means of labor, are, more and more, becoming the property of the capitalists. Those who are despoiled of the means of utilizing in work their own labor-power (or physical capacity for work) are, henceforth, compelled, being unable to live otherwise, to sell the use of that power to the capitalists who hold in their possession the things indispensable for labor. Through their possession of the things indispensable for the functioning of labor-power, the capitalists are, in fact, masters of all who cannot utilize their own power themselves, nor live without utilizing it. From this economic dependence flows the existence of distinct classes, distinct in spite of the civil and political equality of their members; and, as the capitalist regime expropriates the Middle Class more and more, it tends to accentuate the division of society into two principal classes: on the one hand, those who control the means of labor; on the other, those for whom the actual use of those means is the sole possibility of life.

I will ask you to note that I speak of classes and not of orders or estates, because these last expressions imply a legal demarcation between the categories of persons which they indicate; while the word *class* simply denotes, according to Littré,[2] the "grades established among men by the diversity and inequality of their circumstances." This is the reason that some among us refuse to make use of the expression "Fourth Estate." There are no longer any Estates, it is true, but it is not the less true that there still are classes. As no one among us any longer dares to approve of their existence, to deny it is the only way to avoid combatting it. And so it is this denial that is resorted to by those adversaries of socialism whose only weapons are falsehood and hypocrisy. Socialists are not the cause of the existence of classes because they recognize their existence. They limit themselves to establishing that which has been, that which is and that which is destined to be: the origin of classes, their present persistence and their approaching disappearance.

* * *

As soon as, thanks to the development of the faculties of man and to his industrial discoveries, the productivity of labor became great enough for an individual to be able to produce more than was indispensable for his maintenance, the division of society into two great classes, the exploiters and the exploited, was effected. And this division had its justification, so long as production was not sufficient to render comfort for all a possibility. But, thanks to machinery and to scientific appliances which facilitate labor, while vastly multiplying the supply of articles of consumption, the exhausting labor of the masses and the monopolization of comfort by a minority can henceforth give place, must henceforth give place, and will give place in a future which no longer seems distant, to the universalization of labor and its inevitable consequence, the universalization of comfort and of leisure, that is to say, to social conditions under which there will be no classes, because their existence will (as now) serve no useful end as it has done in the past. We will soon see that our present ruling class, far from being useful, is already becoming baneful.

To-day, if the existence of distinct classes has, apparently, lost all legal sanction, it is just as real a fact as ever. To deny it, one must have—pardon me the expression, but I can find no other defining as accurately this state of mind—the desire to play the fool, or the interest to do so. It is impossible to deny seriously that a part of the population is, in fact, through the form of the economic relations, through their material self-interest, through their need of food, placed in a position of dependence upon another portion of the population, and that there is an antagonism between those who must struggle to exist by working and those who can bargain out to them the means of labor.[3]

By proclaiming the existence of classes and their antagonism, by divulging that antagonism, which is not their work, on the political rostrum, socialists are not creating factitious distinctions, they are not resuscitating and do not dream of resuscitating any of the social forms so fortunately and so energetically annihilated by the French Revolution, they are only adapting themselves to the situation as it presents itself to them now.

In fact, modern industry is forcing the workers more and more every day to comprehend the necessity of association or combination in their disputes with the possessors of the means of labor, and thus the interests to be defended have to the workers less and less the false aspect of individual interests; they appear to them in their naked reality as class interests. Born of strikes, of coalitions of every kind imposed upon them by the customs and conditions of life in a capitalist society, their class activity soon takes an a political character. To this then are due the working-class agitations resulting in the recognition of political equality and the establishment of universal suffrage. In possession of political rights, the workingmen are obviously led to make use of these rights in behalf of their own interests. Inevitably, therefore, the political struggle is becoming more and more a class struggle which cannot end until the political power, in the hands of the workingmen, shall at last place the State at the service of the interests of all the exploited, and thus enable the latter to proceed to the economic reforms which will lead to the disappearance of classes as a direct consequence.

Therefore, the Class Struggle is not an invention of the socialists, but the very substance of the facts and acts of history in the making that are daily taking place under their eyes.

III

We know that those whose activity is subordinate in its exercise to a capital which they have not—and these compose the working-class—are compelled to sell their labor-power to some of the possessors of this capital who form, on their side, the bourgeois[4] class.

What is sold by him who has to labor in order to live, and who has not in his possession the means of labor, to the possessor of those means is simply labor in the potential state, that is the muscular or intellectual faculties that must be exerted in the production of useful things. In fact, on the one hand, before these faculties are brought into active exercise, labor does not exist and cannot be sold. Now, the contract is made between the buyer and the seller before any action takes place and has for its effective cause, so far as the seller is concerned, the fact that the seller is so situated that he can not by himself bring his capacity for labor into productive use. On the other hand, as soon as the action (labor) begins, as soon as labor manifests itself, it cannot be the property of the laborer, for it consists in nothing but the incorporation of a thing which the laborer has just alienated by sale—capacity to perform labor—with other things which are not his—the means of production.

To sum up, when the labor does not exist, the laborer can not sell that which he does not possess and which he has not the means of realizing; when the labor does exist, it can not be sold by the laborer to whom it does not belong. The only thing which the laborer can sell is his labor-power, a power distinct from its function, labor, just as the power of marching is distinct from a parade, just as any machine is distinct from its operations.

What is paid under the form of wages by the possessor of the means of labor, the purchaser of the labor-power to the possessor of that power, cannot, therefore, be, and is not, the price of the labor furnished, but is the price of the power made use of, a price that supply and demand cause to oscillate about and especially below its value determined, like the value of any other commodity, by the labor-time socially necessary for its production, or in other words, in this case by the sum which will normally enable the laborer to maintain and perpetuate his labor-power under the conditions necessary for the given kind and stage of production.

But, even when the laborer gets a value equal to the value of his power, he furnishes a value greater than that which he receives. The duration of labor required for a given wage, regularly exceeds the time necessarily occupied by the laborer in adding to the value of the means of production consumed, a value equal to that wage; and the labor thus furnished over and above that which represents the equivalent of what the laborer gets, constitutes *surplus-labor.* Surplus-labor then is unpaid labor.

And here let us be clearly understood. When we speak of unpaid labor, we are stating a simple fact, and do not at all intend to say that capitalists, in the existing state of things, are personally guilty of extracting from the laborers labor for which they do not pay them. We are not of the number of those who think that "the causes of the ills from which we suffer are to be found in men rather than institutions," as M. Glasson declared before the members of the Le Play School. We say exactly the contrary; for us the evil is due to institutions rather than to men and, in society as it is at present constituted, things cannot possibly take place in any other or different fashion.

On the side of the laborer, the thing sold, as I have proved, cannot be his labor. It is his labor-power. The sum paid cannot be the price of his labor. It is the price of his labor-power, a price which, in view of the number of applicants for work, can only very rarely be equal to its value; but, even in this case, he furnishes a greater value than he receives. If he does not, his remuneration is not, strictly speaking, wages, for the furnishing of surplus-labor by the worker is a condition *sine qua non* of wages. When his compensation is split up into wages and supplementary remuneration under the form of profit-sharing or under any other form, the workingman does not furnish less surplus-labor, less unpaid labor; quite the contrary, we may say, for it is clear that this supplementary remuneration, for the laborer, is a mere delusion, mere supplementary moon-shine. All that the workingman can hope to achieve, under, I repeat, the existing organization of society, is the curtailment of his surplus-labor, and that is the explanation and justification of the struggle for the reduction of the working-day, of the Eight Hours movement.

On the side of the capitalist, on account of the fierce war of competition with low prices as weapons which rages throughout the field of production, it is financial suicide for the employer to extract from his work-people less unpaid labor than his competitors do; and that is why it is necessary to strive to obtain the reduction of the day by legal enactment. I add that so long as the employer, so long as the capitalist keeps within the bounds of what may be called the normal conditions of exploitation, he cannot reasonably be held responsible for the economic structure which is so advantageous to him, but which the best of intentions on the part of individuals would be powerless to modify. On the other hand, if capitalists are personally powerless to ameliorate the state of affairs, it would be rash to rush to the conclusion that they are capitalists in the interest of the workers. We must avoid exaggeration in either direction.

Surplus-labor was not invented by the capitalists. Ever since human societies issued from the state of primitive communism, surplus-labor has always existed; and it is the method by which it is wrung from the immediate producers, which differentiates the different economic forms of society.

Before man was able to produce in excess of his needs, one portion of society could not live upon the fruits of the toil of another portion. How could a man work gratuitously for others when his entire time was barely sufficient to procure him his own necessary means of existence? When, in consequence of human progress, labor had acquired such a degree of productiveness that an individual was enabled to produce more than what was strictly necessary for his needs, it became possible for some to subsist upon the toil of others and slavery could be established.

That it was established by force is not doubtful; but it must be confessed that its establishment promoted human evolution. So long as the productiveness of labor, although sufficient to make surplus-labor possible, was not sufficient to render participation in directly useful labor compatible with other occupations or pursuits, the toilsome drudgery and exploitation of some was the necessary condition of the leisure of others, and, thereby, of the development of all. For, if none had had leisure, no progress could have been made in the sciences, the arts and all the branches of knowledge, the benefits of which we all enjoy in some degree. And the fact that the thinkers of antiquity and the greatest among them, Aristotle, excused slavery, is a proof that the mode of thought is determined by the exigencies of the economic organization of society. To reproach Aristotle, in particular, because he did not regard slavery and property as it is natural for us to regard them, is equivalent to reproaching him for not having applied the processes of our modern production to ancient industries.

Slavery did not appear to lack a rational foundation, and did not begin to disappear until the external conditions were profoundly transformed and thus rendered another kind of labor and of surplus-labor more in harmony with the material requirements. Following upon the economic environment in which slavery was the rule there came then the economic environment in which serfdom predominated, and the latter, in its turn, has been superseded by the economic environment in which the wage-system has become the general rule. Each of these environments has had or has its own habits and modes of thought which may be in contradiction with ours, but which are the natural consequences of the modes of life in vogue in their respective eras.

An examination of the aspect of surplus-labor in these three environments shows that it has the appearance of being all labor in the first, a larger or smaller fraction of the whole labor in the second, and apparently falls to zero in the third. In fact, in slavery, during a part of the day, the slave only replaces the value of what he consumes and so really works for himself; notwithstanding, even then his labor appears to be labor for his owner. All his labor has the appearance of surplus-labor, of labor for others. Under serfdom or the *corvée* system, the labor

24

of the serf for himself and his gratuitous labor for his feudal lord are perfectly distinct, the one from the other; by the very way in which the labor is performed, the serf distinguishes the time during which he works for his own benefit from the time which he is compelled to devote to the satisfaction of the wants of his lordly superiors. Under the wage-system, the wage-form, which appears in the guise of direct payment of labor, wipes out every visible line of demarcation between paid labor and unpaid labor; when he receives his wages, the laborer seems to get all the value due to his labor, so that all his labor takes on the form or appearance of paid labor. While, under slavery, the property-relation conceals the labor of the slave for himself, under the wage-system the money-relation conceals the gratuitous labor of the wage-worker for the capitalist. You will readily perceive the practical importance of this disguised appearance of the real relation between labor and capital. The latter is deemed to breed or expand by its own virtue, and the former to receive its full remuneration.

IV

Wage-labor as an economic form existed before the actual appearance of industrial capital which in fact only dates from the day when production by the aid of wage-labor became general. Capital, in fact, is not a quality with which the means of production are naturally endowed, which they have always had and which they are destined always to have. It is a character which they possess only under definite social conditions. The means of production are no more naturally capital than a negro is naturally a slave. And when socialists talk of suppressing capital and capitalists, those who do not wish to make a ridiculous confusion, ought to remember that it is simply a question of taking away from the means of production and those who hold possession of them a character which they now have, and which can be taken from them without destroying an atom of their material substance, just as in suppressing slavery, it is not necessary, in order to take away the slave-character from the negro, to kill the negro.

For a long time capital was known only under the form of merchants' capital and usurers' capital; for it was only, or almost only, under those two forms that money bred its like, and it is this possibility of money's breeding which constitutes capital. This possibility could not exist, except as an exceptional fact, for money invested in the means of production, so long as industry remained more or less domestic in character. In order for capital to spread beyond the domain of commerce in goods and money and appear in the domain of production, it was necessary for the wealth accumulated in commerce and usury to effect on a large scale the concentration of the scattered petty producers and their petty individual tools; the workshop had to be enlarged; it was necessary to bring together a large number of workers working at the same time, in the same place, under the orders of the same "captain of industry," in producing on a large scale the same kind of commodity, and to find for the disposal of the latter a sufficiently extended market.

The money advanced in production can, in fact, realize an appreciable profit by the sale of the objects produced, only when its possessor is able to realize a certain quantity of surplus-labor; now, to accomplish this he must have a certain number of laborers. For it is the surplus-labor realized, we know, that forms the excess of the value produced over that of the money laid out in production, or, in other words, the surplus-value which incessantly swells the capital and continually increases its power to dominate labor.

The capitalist mode of production, the mode of production in which the means of labor function as capital, owes to capital its specific character, which is its power of making money breed money, of giving birth to surplus-value. The capitalist purchaser of labor-power has only one object, viz., to enrich himself by making his money breed or expand, by the process of making commodities containing more labor than he pays for, and by selling which he therefore realizes a value greater than that of the sum of the advances or outlays made.

If, since the productiveness of labor has made it possible, one part of society has, under various economic forms, been forced to add to the labor-time required for its own support, a certain amount of surplus-labor-time, for which it has received no equivalent and the benefit of which has been enjoyed by another part of society, it is likewise true that so long as the aim of production was to enable the privileged class to appropriate the means of consumption and enjoyment, the surplus-labor of the immediate producers reached its limit with the full satisfaction of those needs and desires, as extensive as they might be, to gratify which was the object of this appropriation. But as soon as it becomes a question of obtaining, instead of a certain mass of products, the production at any cost of surplus-value, the incessant multiplication of money, the possessor of the means of production strives relentlessly to make those means of production absorb the greatest possible quantity of surplus-labor.

If this insatiable thirst for and headlong pursuit of surplus-value has been for the laborers and their families the cause of an exploitation of their labor-power, more burdensome than any form of exploitation previously known, it must be recognized that it has contributed to the development of the means of production. It is with capital as with slavery. Both, sources of sufferings for their victims, they have been, on the whole, sources of progress for humanity. The history of human progress is far from being an idyl. Our too forgetful and too proud civilization is the result of a long series of torments and miseries endured by the nameless and forgotten masses.

Therefore capital has had its utility, and the era of capitalist production constitutes a great step forward in the evolution of the productive powers. Beginning with the enlargement of the small guild workshop, passing through action in common, the co-operation of a large number of laborers in the enlarged workshop through the manufacturing stage, by the division of labor within the workshop, by the introduction and general adoption of the machine-tool, by the employment of steam as a motive power, capitalist production has finally developed into modern mechanical industry which has revolutionized the mode of production more radically than had any previous change. It is its continuous and radical alteration of the technical processes which distinguishes the capitalist period from all the preceding periods, and prevents it from having the relatively permanent conservative character which they had.

V

What are the results of these revolutions in industrial methods, and what are their tendencies?

Machinery is more and more seizing upon all industries, and, instead of making use of his tool, the laborer is the servant of the machine. The relative ease of work of this kind makes it possible to substitute unskilled labor for skilled labor, women and children for men. By thus throwing men out of work, the instrument of labor lowers wages and expropriates the laborer from his means of existence. This machinery, thanks to which the genius of Aristotle foresaw the possibility of the emancipation of the slave, has as yet been merely a cause of enslavement, and just as man is moulded by the economic environment which is his own work, he is here enslaved by his own product.

With the extension of the system of mechanical industry, the product ceases more and more to be the work of an individual. The individual by himself alone no longer makes a product, but a fraction of a product, and the owner no longer works with his instrument of labor, or, in other words, uses his property himself, but turns this task over to a certain number of laborers, to a group of wage-slaves. Thus, when the possessor of a hand-saw works with it, the owner uses his own property;

with the machine-saw, it is used not by the owner, but by the laborers, whom he has to employ to operate it. While the operation of the means of production so largely augmented requires the common action of a host of workers, the undertakings and establishments grow to such dimensions that the vast sums of capital necessary for their conduct are not to be found in the hands of a single capitalist. Having become too gigantic for a single capitalist, the title or nominal ownership of these means of production, and along with it the profits, passes from the individual capitalist to an association of capitalists, to a company of stockholders. This company actually has, considered as a collective body, a particular tangible property; but what does this property represent for each individual shareholder? A fiction. The individual stockholder cannot lay his finger upon any particular material object and say: that is mine.

While the means of production are thus ceasing to be in the strict sense private property, and require for their actual operation a collective body of laborers, while the product is becoming a social product, the owners of the means of production and the products, are becoming shareholders, and thus ceasing to perform any useful function, to have any real utility. The success of a business in former times depended upon the energy and skill of its proprietor, just as it sometimes does to-day in small manufacturing or mercantile establishments. Since the introduction of stock companies, the producing organism is no longer affected by the personal traits of those who own it; it does not know the shareholder, the present knows his property; it functions independently of him, and does not feel his influence, so that even a change of ownership has no effect upon it. The former functions of the proprietor are at the present time performed by wage-workers, trained engineers or managers, more or less well paid, but still wage-workers. In place of the managing proprietor, we have then a salaried manager, and he is a better manager because he is only a salaried employee, as M. de Molinari admits, when he writes:

"All that is requisite is for him to possess the ability, knowledge and character demanded for his functions, and these are all qualities which are more easily and cheaply obtained on the market, divorced from capital than united to it."[5]

Not only is the proprietary class, "the haves," losing all social utility, but, more than this, it is becoming baneful through its exclusive pre-occupation with personal profits. Baneful it is henceforth for all branches of social production which the mad and unorganized pursuit of profits subjects to disastrous perturbations, to periodical crises swamping the market and lasting amid failures and shut-downs until the outlets for goods once more open up; baneful for all the workers, worked to utter exhaustion in periods of business activity and reduced to wretched poverty in periods of industrial depression, during which they suffer from want of everything, because there is, relatively to the purchasing power of the people, too much of everything—(here we see once more the creator dominated by the creation, the producers by their products, just as in the cases formerly noticed of the human intelligence and the economic environment, of the machine and the workman); baneful for all consumers, who are victims of the adulteration of products begotten by the mad strife for gain; baneful for the petty capitalists, the small producers in constant danger of bankruptcy and ruin through the intensity of the war of competition which always results in the victory of the great capitalists or the great combinations of capital (trusts, etc.).

To recapitulate, our economic movement tends toward labor in common, since the operation of the means of production is passing from the working-proprietor to a collective group of laborers, and toward the elimination of the mode or form of private or individual ownership of the means of production, since the nominal property in them is passing from the individual proprietor to a collective body of shareholders (stock-company or trust). It also tends to leave the proprietary class no useful role or function, thus making them for the future not only superfluous, but baneful.

At the same time that the organization of labor adapted to the present form and state of the productive forces is escaping from the hands of the proprietary class and is thus the signal that the close of its historic career is at hand, it is concentrating and organizing men everywhere in the same way that it concentrates material wealth. It brings the laborers together and leads them, through their identity in position and interests, to combine in groups or unions, it constitutes them into a class more and more conscious of its situation, disciplines their masses systematically arranged and graded in each industrial establishment, and fashions out of their own ranks an intellectual aristocracy upon which devolves the function of super-intending and managing all industries.

And while the individual form of their petty tools or instruments of labor, and their mode of production which keeps them in independent isolation, engender in the workers in petty industries ideas too individualistic and egoistic, wherever modern mechanical industry has already wrested from the laborer his tool and transformed it into a mechanical apparatus effacing individuality from the labor-process, wherever individual labor merges into and blends with collective labor, wherever the technical processes are such that the task of each is of service only through the participation (co-operation) of all, and is itself the condition of the performance of the collective task, the strictly individualistic tendencies of the producers in the petty industries are replaced by the spirit of solidarity, which, with the progress of industrial development, is leading— nay, forcing the working class every day more and more toward socialist ideas, ideas which spring from the material necessities which inexorably force their way into the minds of men.

These are facts against which our personal preferences are of no avail. The material and intellectual elements of the collective (or co-operative) form of production, elaborated by the capitalist regime, are thus developing more and more every day, and socialism is, you see, the natural consequence of existent conditions. It is not something imported from abroad and added to our social movement, neither is it an article of export good for any sort of economic environment; it is the rigorous consequence of a certain orderly sequence of facts, the result of a definite evolution whose progress it has noted, but which has taken place independently of it; it has not created it because it has been conscious of its existence.

And so, as M. Paul Leroy-Beaulieu recognizes: "the field of modern mechanical industry is extending its boundaries more and more, and it is difficult to see what limits can be set to its possible extension." Now it is modern industry which lays bare the antagonisms immanent in capitalist production, and at the same time renders their destruction possible. The historic role of capital has been the development of the productive powers, and, in the process of developing them, it has created the weapons which are destined to kill it. Necessary during a certain stage of economic development, it is not eternal, but inevitably comes to an end with a change in the relations of the means of production to the producers.

VI

The preparation and training of the working-class (for their high functions) by the productive powers, the growing and inevitable development and crystallization of the collective tendencies of the latter, the increasing incompatibility between their essential character and their private ownership, all lead to a new economic regime in which they will be owned and controlled collectively just as they are operated collectively, in which they will be conducted by society and for society. And all the socialism of the socialists consists of wishing to perpetuate in a fully developed form the present social character of the material conditions of life.

I say socialism of the socialists because we have seen flourish in our day a peculiar socialism, the socialism of those good people who earnestly wish to remove the inconveniences and injustices of our present social state, but who also wish a little more earnestly to preserve the cause of these inconveniences, who wish at once to suppress or abolish the proletariat and to preserve the capitalist form of society. It is quite possible for socialism also to have its converts and even its backsliders; it asks its adherents, not whence they come, but to go whither it is going, or, at least, to permit it to proceed upon its road without attempting to turn it aside from it. As one of our adversaries declares, we can say in our turn: 'On one side are the socialists, on the other those who are not socialists,' and among the latter may be counted those who accept the name while rejecting the thing.

Apart from the socialization of the means of labor which have already taken on a collective form, there may be and there often is charlatanry, but there is no real possibility of emancipation, there is no socialism.

So long as the means of labor and labor shall not be united in the same hands, the means of labor will retain the character of capital, and capital will inevitably exploit the workingman and wring from him labor for which it will not pay him. The source of the troubles of the working-class is to be found in their expropriation from the means of labor; now, the harder they work on the established basis of expropriation, the more power they give the capitalist class to enrich themselves and to expropriate those who have not yet entered the inner circle of capitalism. On the basis of the present gigantic forms of the instruments of labor, the collective means of labor and labor itself can be united in the same hands, only by the transformation of the capitalist ownership of these means of labor into social ownership, only by the transformation of capitalist production into social production. The logical consequence of the material facts of the existing environment, this transformation, the socialization of the means of production having collective tendencies, is possible, and it appears as the only practical method of emancipating the laborers, of emancipating society as a whole.

Emancipated the laborers will be, since their lives will no longer be dependent upon the means of labor monopolized by others and they will be free to make their lives what they will. In fact, they will freely choose the kind of productive labor they prefer, and all kinds of work will, in accordance with the law of supply and demand, be reduced in varying proportions to definite quantities of ordinary labor. After once deducting from the product of the labor of each a portion which will take the place of the present taxes, the portion necessary to replace the means of labor consumed, to provide for the extension of the scale of production, for insurance against disastrous contingencies, such, for instance, as floods, lightning, tornadoes, etc., for the support of those incapable of labor, to meet generously the expenses of administration and of satisfying the common requirements of sanitation, education, etc., the producers of both sexes will distribute the balance among themselves, proportionally to the quantity of ordinary labor furnished by them severally. The right of each laborer will be equal, in the sense that for all, without distinction, the labor furnished will be the measure alike for all, and this equal right may possibly lead to an unequal distribution, according to the greater or smaller quantities of labor furnished. The standard of rights in force in an economic environment cannot be superior in quality to that environment, but it will go on increasing in perfection as the environment advances toward perfection, thus reducing, so far as material conditions shall permit, the inequalities of natural origin.

The important point is that, from the dawn of social production, there will be no more surplus-labor, no more classes, and, therefore, no more exploitation, as there inevitably is under capitalist production. Every adult able to work will receive, under one form or another, partly in articles for personal consumption, partly in social guarantees, in public services of every kind, the same quantity of labor that he shall give to society. If goods are rationed out, this rationing will not be accompanied by exploitation; as rationing can then be due only to a deficiency in personal or social production, and not to the spoliation which the wage-system implies, a system under which overproduction, far from being favorable to the satisfaction of the demand of the working-class for articles of consumption, results for them in loss of employment and starvation diet.

During the capitalist period, it suffices for socialism to establish the possibility of the emancipation of the working-class and to work for that emancipation. There is no occasion to waste time in working out and settling the details of the organization of the future society. Each epoch has its task. Let us not have the presumption to lay down rules for those who are to come after us, and let us be content with present duties. The point upon which socialism trains its guns at present, though recognizing the utility that it has had in the past, is the capital-form; but let us not forget that the substance beneath this form will be every whit preserved. When an office is taken away from an office-holder, the individual is left without a hair the less. In the same way, in taking from the means of production their function as capital, everything that functions to-day under that form will remain intact. Socialism then attacks the capital-form, the form only, and it attacks it only in so far as the economic phenomena authorize such an attack. Everything which constitutes the substance of capital will be preserved, the capital-form alone will disappear and along with it that power that it involves of exploiting the labor of others.

What will be the fate of the capitalists?

Capital appears to be a collective power or force, by its origin, since it springs from the accumulated surplus-labor of a collective body of laborers, by its functional activity since it also requires a collective body of laborers to enable it to enter upon its functions, and by its mode of ownership since, if it is private property, it tends more and more to be the private property, not of an individual, but of a collective body, a company or trust. To make public property of the means of production, which are capital when they are able to exploit the labor of others and which are capital only on that condition, is simply to generalize the collective or social character which they already have.

Is the holder of a share in a mining or railway company or any sort of stock-company justified in speaking of "his" property? Where is his property? In what does it consist? What can he show if someone asks to see it? A machine? A piece of real estate? No, simply one or several bits of paper which represent only an infinitesimal fraction of an undivided whole. Would this shareholder be any the less a property-owner, if this undivided whole should become an integrant portion of the national property? Would there be such a great difference between "his" property, as it now is, and his quota or share in the national property? Just as the capitalists understand well enough to-day how to avail themselves of the national forests, for instance, for fresh air, pleasure excursions afoot and awheel, recreation, etc., so, after the socialization of the material objects that make up what is at present capital, they would use this newly nationalized property as means of labor or production.

This, then, would be a true democratization[6] of property. The process, ordinarily called by this name, the dispersion of shares, stocks and bonds, is only the process—called legitimate—of extracting good hard cash from all pockets, even those most scantily supplied, centralizing it, monopolizing the real possession of it in exchange for a certificate of nominal ownership, making it breed or expand, and permitting to flow back in interest, dividends, etc., only tiny crumbs until the day comes when the poor investors cease to get even these microscopical returns. This pretended democratization of property results simply in the formation of a financial aristocracy creating scandalous fortunes out of the good dollars of the small investors, and if these dollars, when the paper accepted in their stead is no longer worth anything, are lost for their former possessors, they are not lost for everyone. (They have become the reward of "abstinence."—

Translator.)

Let the stocks representing part-ownership in a company lose all value—this is an occurrence that the shareholders and bondholders of the Panama canal, for example, can tell you is not unknown in our bourgeois society—and the shareholder finds himself, in this instance, permitted to enjoy all the blessings of expropriation without any indemnifying compensation; sometimes even he has the delicate attention of an invitation from the Receiver or the Courts to pour some more money into the hole where his former savings disappeared. Now even in this case the owners of this sort of personal property do not make too much ado about the matter. Why should they complain any more bitterly on the day when there will be, as it were, only a substitution of one kind of stocks or shares for another, when they will all become stockholders and bondholders of the great society (the Co-operative Commonwealth), instead of being shareholders and bondholders in one or several little societies or companies?

By this transformation they will gain complete assurance against risk of loss—a real enough danger to-day when, after the actual control of property passes into the hands of financial magnates, the revenue of the nominal owners, the stockholders, etc., falls to zero or nearly zero, thus cutting off their means of existence or enjoyment. They will lose only one thing: the power of dominating the labor of others and of appropriating its fruits; while they will have the privilege of enjoying the common wealth and the advantages springing from its co-operative employment.

Healthy adults will take for their own use, provided they work, their share of the social products. If they are already accustomed to any kind of work, they will find no hardship in this obligation to perform useful labor; if they are not accustomed to it, they will acquire the habit and will find their health greatly improved thereby in every respect. If they are old and infirm they will be liberally provided for by society.

37

What they can reasonably expect and insist upon having is the sustenance of life (in a broad sense),[7] and this they will have, as you see, in any case. The socialization will not result in such a change in the distribution of wealth as is often caused by watering the stock of a company. It will simply extend to all, those who hold stocks at present included, those advantages which a minority alone enjoys to-day, and it will benefit all, but stockholders especially, by doing away with those risks which capitalist exploitation forces everyone to run.

* * *

Finally, socialism will rob no one. I would ask those who assert the contrary, what description then should be given to those transactions in the goods and property of the nobility, the clergy and above all of the communes, performed by our great radicals in the French Revolution, by those whose work has become a "compass" for our guidance. Just as soon as we cease simply substituting one privileged class for another, just as soon as we enable all without exception to enjoy the same advantages, no one will be robbed or deprived of anything. Simply, inequality in the enjoyment of privilege will have been abolished, another privileged class will have vanished from the stage. Yes, the capitalists will lose, along with their special privileges or rights over the means of production, that characteristic or quality that makes them capitalists; but, I repeat, they will have exactly the same rights as all others to the use and enjoyment of those means of production, from that time forth the inalienable property of society. With capital dethroned, the principles of the Republic will at last be applied with controlling power to the field of economics, just as they are to the field of politics, and political democracy will have ceased to be a farce, for it will have developed into its perfect flower, Industrial Democracy.

VII

Far from being a material upheaval, the advent of socialism will be simply the culmination of the economic evolution now going on. Born, in its contemporaneous form, from the study of facts, socialism sees in the facts the controlling elements of the modifications to be effected. It makes no pretence of going in advance of the economic phenomena, it limits itself to following them, to adapting itself to conditions which it does not create and which it is not its part to create. Now, if, in all those cases where the means of production are already collectively owned by companies or trusts or are concentrated in the hands of single individuals, they can be placed at the disposition of ALL only by the substitution of society as a whole for their present capitalist possessors, in those cases in which the form of ownership of the means of labor is still truly individual, *i.e.*, where they are still in the hands of those who themselves directly make use of them in actual work, it is not for society to force itself into the place of the present proprietors. The purpose of the interference of society, indeed, is to give, in the only form to-day possible, the means of production to the laborers who have them not, it is to restore the tools and materials of labor to those who have been robbed of them. It is not its business, then, to interfere in those cases where the laborers are still in possession of their tools and materials. And so the peasant will retain the patch of land he possesses and tills, the petty tools and implements will continue to belong to the artisan-manufacturer who himself works with them, until the facts shall lead them to renounce voluntarily this form of private ownership, no longer to their advantage, in order to enjoy the far more fruitful benefits of collective ownership and production.

Moreover, just as, in the capitalist period, the changes brought about by the development of machinery re-acted upon even those branches of production in which machinery had not

39

as yet been introduced, by developing, for example, in all branches the exploitation of women and children, in the same way, the advantages of the socialization of the means of production previously centralized by the capitalists, will re-act upon the petty proprietors of the means of production not yet socialized. The petty producer, who remains master of his own instrument of labor, will, through the simultaneity and propinquity of the embryonic co-operative commonwealth, get the help he needs. Notably, he will be freed from the clutches of the financial middlemen whose victim he is at present; his labor, freed from their exploitation, will be in its turn emancipated, just as truly, although in a different way, as will be the labor of those who, exploited to-day because they lack the means of labor, will have these means, socialized, placed at their free disposition. The result for all will thus be the emancipation of labor, in the one case, by placing the socialized means of labor at the free disposition of all laborers, in the other, by leaving to the individual laborer his individual tool. In both cases, the tools will be owned by those who use them.

And, though it displeases our opponents, this way of proceeding is very logical, although it does not conform to their pretended conception of logic. The logic of the Socialists does not consist in forcing a solution demanded by a certain set of facts upon other facts which do not yet require that solution, it does not consist in making fish live out of the water because that mode of life agrees with men. It consists in adapting itself in all cases to the environment, to the facts, in always acting with reference to the facts, instead of requiring the same kind of action in the face of different combinations of facts. To those who assert that this position is in conflict with the "pure dogma of the socialist church," you have only to reply that there is neither a socialist church nor a socialist dogma, but that there are far too many bourgeois imbeciles who attempt to palm off ideas made by themselves out of the whole cloth as the dogmas of socialism.

During the sixteen years that our socialist theory has

been developing in France, it has never varied upon the subject of the petty producers. Those who assert the contrary follow their own imaginations and not the facts. I defy them to prove that we have not always spoken in the same way in regard, for example, to the small farms of the peasants. They now accuse our opinion on this subject of opportunism, using the word in its political meaning; they could, more correctly, accuse us of having always professed opportunism, but this time using the word in the sense implied by its derivation. You know how necessary it is to avoid the confusion—opportune for some, it is true—of the political meaning of a word with its true meaning. The political radicals are far from being radical in the ordinary sense, and their brothers (nominally opponents) the opportunists, instead of wishing that which is opportune, find nothing opportune except the satisfaction of their own appetites and the postponement of all else. In the true meaning—the time has come to say it—of the word, there cannot be a party more thoroughly opportunist than the socialist party which—I will not cease repeating—must simply adapt itself to the facts and which has no guide, save the facts, to point the way in the transformation of property.

When we talk of the transformation of property which is nothing, as they are obliged to confess, but "a social institution,"[8] our opponents, with their strange fashion of doing us justice, change our words into "suppression of property." "Socialists of all schools have decreed the suppression of property"[9] is the notable affirmation of "a certain number of young men, strangers hitherto to politics"[10] —this part of the phrase is not mine, it is, possibly, the least open to criticism of any part of the work of the young men in question, who have felt impelled to speak on a question that they confess is foreign to them. Their confession is superfluous; we would have readily perceived, unaided, that they spoke of socialism after the fashion of those who know nothing of it.

These young men, in founding the *"comité d'action de la gauche libérale,"*[11] wrote: "We are partisans of individual liberty and of individual property." I assume, until proof to the contrary is forthcoming, that they are not partisans of these things for themselves and their friends alone. If they advocate them for every one, I beg them to tell us what they think of the liberty of the man who has, as his source of livelihood, only his labor-power without the means of utilizing it.

Either they recognize that every man ought to have the means of labor at his disposal, and, in that case, I will ask them how, with the system of mechanical industry, they hope to put at the disposal of all these means so necessary to the liberty of all.

Or, they do not recognize that every man, to be free, must dispose of the tools and materials of labor, and then I will ask them what becomes of the liberty of the man to whom the employer can say: if you do such or such a thing, if you do not accept such or such a thing, you shall have no work, that is to say, it shall be impossible for you to eat. And that they may not accuse me of describing hypothetical cases blacker than nature, I will submit for their meditation the following fact related by the *Temps* (Times)[12] at the time of the strike of Rive-de-Gier.

"An engine-stoker fell ill. He was replaced, all the time of his illness, by a common laborer at 50 cents a day. The regular stoker having gotten well, resumed his duties. He was completely surprised, at the end of the fortnight, to receive only 50 cents a day, when he had been paid, before his illness, 80 cents. He protested. 'There it is. Take it or leave it,' he was told; 'we have found out that a common laborer at 50 cents does this work just as well as you; we cut you down to 50 cents. Get out or accept it.' The man had a family, and choice was forbidden him. He accepted it."

In the face of such facts, M. Célestin Jonnart has the assurance—which I will describe, returning one of the epithets he applies to us, as "villainous"—to assert that the socialists "are working for conditions which will produce generations of men who will know nothing but abject submission and will be ready for every degradation." These generations, sir, are not to

42

be made; they are to be raised from their degradation, and that is the task at which socialism is working.

If I have cited only one fact, this is not because facts of this kind are rare, it is because the one I have cited has the advantage of coming from the *Temps* which may be suspected of anything you like except socialism. Then, besides proving how free the laborer is in his choice, this fact shows how the free contract between capitalist and laborer is concluded. When the stoker resumes his place, he naturally imagines that he is resuming it upon the former conditions, and no one undeceives him. On pay-day, which does not come till a fortnight later, he perceives that he must conclude a new free contract different from the one he had a right to believe in force, and accept 50 cents instead of the 80 cents expected and agreed upon.

Are these men free, the stoker and his like? I would gladly have on this point the opinion of M. Léon Say who not long since posed as the champion, against the socialists, of "human liberty and dignity." The truth is that the laborer is free, only when, to the right of being free, he joins the effective power of being free, only when he has at his disposition the things necessary to the realization of his labor, only, in other words, when he does not have to throw himself upon the mercy of the possessors of those things. Whatever the law may say, the man who depends upon another for his subsistence is not free. What is requisite is to furnish means of labor to the laborers who have them not; now, on the basis of the present form or character of these means, society can assure possession of them to all, only when these means shall have been socialized, shall have become social property. As regards the laborers who still possess their means of labor, they will retain them, as I explained just above. In fact, only through socialism can individual liberty be made a reality for all.

It is the same with individual property as with individual liberty. From all that I have just stated it is clear that the only property that socialism wishes to transform, is the property no

43

longer made use of by the individual owners thereof; it is the property which is formed by the agglomeration of petty scraps of property wrested from the immense majority, and which exists only to the detriment of that very majority.[13] And even in this case there will be no suppression, since the present holders will be granted the use of their transformed property on the same terms as others.

What, then, is the property of "those silent multitudes who toil and struggle so hard for existence and who are in truth the artisans of our greatness?"[14] Is not your capitalist society stripping them more and more every day of the means of labor and of individually owned dwellings, and leaving to them in individual ownership only the things indispensable to the bare support of life? It is the capitalist regime which, by increasing immeasurably the property of the few, contracts the limits within which the personal acquirement of property by the many is possible. It is the socialist regime which will increase this possibility of the personal acquirement of property, by assuring to each the share earned by his labor. It is only under the regime of socialism that individual property will be a reality for all, as this regime alone will suppress—though suppressing nothing else—the possibility of using this property to exploit the labor of others.

VIII

It appears that from the moment when it will no longer be possible to exploit the individual, there will no longer be any individuality. At least it so appears to the capitalists who deem that which does not yield them a profit to be non-existent. To the socialists, on the other hand, the existence of individuality appears dependent upon its freedom. Now, as it is, as we have just seen, only in the socialist period that all individuals will be able to have the means necessary to true freedom, it follows that the triumph of socialism will be the triumph of the individual, the blossoming of personality.[15] In the socialist period, indeed, all those who shall wish to work will be able to do so, by choosing freely their favorite kind of socially useful labor, and all will be able to consume the social products proportionally to the labor they have furnished. Will it not, therefore, be to the interest of all to work, and to try to make the work as little toilsome and as productive as possible? Is there not here, apart from the joy of serving one's fellows, the most powerful motive for emulation both as regards the quantity of labor individually performed and in the invention or discovery of improved processes tending to procure for each and all the maximum of benefits in return for the minimum of exertion?

A certain degree of audacity is required to dare compare the producers of the future under socialism, with the office-holders of to-day under capitalism. What interest has the office-holder of to-day to reduce to the minimum the cost to the State of the services it is his function to perform? His salary, determined before any labor is performed, is independent of the quantity and quality of his labor; and so the office-holder, though full of righteous indignation against the workingmen who wish to work only eight hours a day, seeks, on his own part, to work just as little as possible, and he squanders and wastes as much as possible, because extravagance never costs him a penny and sometimes brings him in handsome rewards. While under the regime of socialism, the personal interest of the individual will be in harmony with the social interest of all, under the present system the personal interests of the office-holders are in direct conflict with the interest of the State. Under the regime of socialism, men, all men, will be producers and not office-holders; they will not be office-holders any more than are members of a family who, in order to provide for the satisfaction of the needs of the family, perform severally various functions.

* * *

In conclusion, the whole question may be summed up

thus: Is the spirit of initiative and personal energy likely to be more broadly disseminated among the masses, when the latter know that they are compelled to make their own wretchedness the instrument of the prosperity of a minority, or when they shall know that their own prosperity will be whatever they, by their own labor, shall make it, under a system of absolute equality of privilege? There can be no doubt as to the answer in the minds of all those who are not too much wonted to the denial of truth. But, under the regime of socialism, initiative[16] and energy cannot promote personal interests alone; while being more favorable than ever to those interests, they will necessarily be advantageous to all. As soon as the material conditions necessary for the attainment of individual prosperity shall also be the conditions requisite for social prosperity, we shall see grow out of this harmony a system of ethics based on the newly acquired consciousness of social solidarity, and under this new morality the action of the individual will have not only as its necessary though indirect result, but also as its guiding principle, motive and goal, the social or common interest, the greatest good of all.

It would seem that from this time forth all ought to unite their efforts in order to hasten the dawn of the realization of a social environment so advantageous to all. In fact, excepting a very small minority of great financiers and capitalists, all those who work or have worked with hand or brain, all have an interest in the triumph of socialism; unfortunately all are not conscious of the undeniable precariousness of the situation of all under the regime of capitalism, and so do not see the advantage for all in transforming this regime along the lines of its social tendencies, and many will stupidly strive to prolong the state of things which is the cause of their troubles.

Socialism repels no one and is open to all those, without regard to their social position, who comprehend its necessity. But, if it is far from repelling them—striving indeed to attract them—it cannot count in advance, generally speaking, on those who too readily become the dupes of illusions begotten by a more or less privileged social situation and who are unable to rise above their class prejudices sufficiently to form a just conception of their own true interests. While preparing the ground for socialism which is developing wherever the capitalist mode of production has reached a certain stage, the economic phenomena at the same time necessitate the economic and political organization of the industrial[17] laborers, and they are the class immediately and directly interested in the triumph of socialism.

Small industrial employers, artisans, retail merchants and working owners of small farms have two-fold class-ties. They belong to the possessing class, and yet they are exploited. When, under the empire of a naive pride and vain hopes, the man proud of his possessions, the would-be capitalist, dominates in them, they give heed to the dirty blackguards who are forever telling them that the common laborer and the socialist wish to take their little property away from them, and they show a hostility which, in spite of their conservative intentions, is aimed against those whom they ought to help if they wish to be sure of retaining the little property they have. When, under the lashes of the thong of stern reality they feel themselves exploited and menaced with expropriation, they applaud the demands of the socialists and help support—as has often been seen—the strikes of the laborers. According to circumstances the middle class declares itself in this way, now on one side, now on the other.

The industrial workingmen who own nothing but their labor-power and to whom the possession, even in a dream, of the smallest estate is an impossibility, cannot possibly conceive the false idea that they have anything to lose by the victory of socialism. From that to thinking that they have everything to gain by that victory is not far; for this all that is needed is for them to be brought into contact with the socialist propaganda. Therefore the principal mission of socialism is to instruct and organize the multitudes of industrial laborers; they must be won over the first of all. This which is, in fact, for the middle class only a defensive war against the great capitalists becomes an offensive war for the great majority of the industrial laborers who have to conquer that which the middle class has only to preserve.

Because we say that socialism makes its appeal more particularly to the industrial laborers, we beg our critics not to represent us as saying that socialism ought to neglect the members of all other classes. Socialism struggling for the emancipation—no longer impossible—of all, combats in every rank or stratum of society all exploitations and all oppressions, and it is the natural defender of all the exploited and all the oppressed. Just as, to regard the economic question as the sum and substance of militant socialism is not, in our opinion, to restrict its field of action, but is simply, on the contrary, to pursue directly the only line of conduct by which it is possible for its efforts to produce broad general effects, so to devote our attention first of all to the industrial laborers is not to make light of the wrongs of the other victims of exploitation, but it is to devote our first efforts to strengthening the active army of socialism, formed of those who have to blaze out a path for the movement, but whose success—which will be hastened by the support of members of other classes—will assure the emancipation of all.

IX

Socialism and the party which incarnates it are begotten by the economic transformations which are taking place under our eyes. If it is impossible to suppress (or eliminate) certain phases of social development, at a certain stage of development it is possible for men to facilitate or retard the success of socialism. This depends sometimes upon men who are not socialists, and nearly always upon socialist tactics.

Is socialism inexorably destined to wait for "the natural play (working) of institutions and laws to bring to pass the triumph of its aspirations," as M. Charles Dupuy asked in one of

48

his astonishing addresses? Socialism which is essentially an evolutionary theory expects its realization to result from the natural working out of the facts; but, under normal conditions, it can no more rely on the natural play or action of existing laws, than a republican, eager for the Republic, could with any show of reason, have relied, in the time of the Empire, on the natural working of the imperial laws to evolve the Republic. But in a republic, such as France or the United States, where universal suffrage makes the People the sole nominal sovereign, and where by strictly legal action the People may become the effective, actual sovereign, if socialism cannot rely for its triumph upon the free play and natural working of the laws of evolution, it can rely upon the ever-growing influence of socialist electors and officials on political action and legislation —a source of hope that was forbidden to the republicans under the empire. It may also happen that its triumph may be brought about by a rupture of *de facto* legality, a rupture which under certain contingencies may become unavoidable, a rupture which may be forced upon them without any regard to the personal preferences of socialists, as, for example, in France, on the 4th of September, 1870, such a rupture was forced upon Jules Simon and other fanatical partisans of legality, and it is a rupture of this kind which constitutes a revolution.

Evolution and Revolution are not contradictory terms. Quite the contrary. When they both take place, the one following and supplementing the other, the second is the conclusion of the first, the revolution is only the characteristic crisis which ends and gives real effect to a period of evolution. Notice what takes place in the case of the young chick. After having gone through the regular process of development inside of its shell, the little brute, who is as yet unable to read the *Temps*, does not know that it has been decreed that evolution must take place without any violence; instead of employing its leisure in gently and legally wearing a hole through its shell, it breaks its way out without warning or ceremony. Well, then, socialism which does read the *Temps*, will act just as though it had not read it, and, if the emergency arises, will imitate the little chick; if in the course of events it becomes necessary, it will burst asunder the mould of legality within which it is developing, and within which, at the present time, it has simply to continue its regular and peaceful development.

The distinctive mark of a revolution, as I have said, is the rupture of *de facto* legality—that is the only *sine qua non*, everything else is merely incidental. Unfortunately the strong general tendency is to think that the word, revolution, necessarily implies the execution of persons and the destruction of property. The latter are catastrophes that the socialists will make every possible effort to avoid; for they know that excesses in one direction inevitably provoke a re-actionary movement in the opposite direction, and they will do everything they possibly can to keep from thus unconsciously defeating their own ends.

At some particular time in the future events may occur that, purely by the power of circumstances over men, will lead to a rupture of legality. When and how will this happen, if it does happen? We know nothing about it, and we are not and will not be the responsible cause of such an event, because we recognize and point out the possibility of its occurrence. The interested fears of some will not destroy this possibility, nor will the too pardonable impatience of others convert it into a probability. As the *Temps* said one day, in speaking incidentally of revolutions: "One does not make them; they make themselves."[18]

Although we can not indicate the character any more than the period of this possible rupture of legality, still we have a right to say that this rupture, or in other words, this revolution, may take place peacefully, like the one that occurred on the 4th of September, 1870. The difference in the consequences of the two revolutions makes no difference from our present point of view. It is true that the revolution of the 4th of September was purely a political revolution. But, while the revolution, whose possibility we are considering, is to usher in a social transformation, as a revolution it is simply a change of a political character. If the capitalists are as prudent as were the Bonapartists on the 4th of September, the future rupture of legality may be just as peaceful as was that in which Senator Jules Simon took part. It is seen, then, that socialism may burst the mould of legality while preserving the peace. On the other hand, it may make use of violence while remaining within the forms of strict legality.

Whether or not a revolutionary situation is destined to arise, the duty, the whole duty of socialists consists in educating the masses, in rendering them conscious of their condition, their task and their responsibility, of organizing them in readiness for the day when the political power shall fall into their hands. To win for socialism the greatest possible number of partisans, that is the task to which socialist parties must consecrate their efforts, using, for this purpose, all pacific and legal means, but using such means only. In ordinary times, such as those in which we live, any sort of action, except peaceful and legal action with a view to the instruction and organization of the masses, is sure, whether so intended or not, to have a deterrent and reactionary influence, and to interfere with the spread of socialist ideas.

What I am advocating is not the policy of keeping our colors hidden in our pockets, it is not the policy of mutilating, however slightly, the theory of socialism, it is the policy of sticking strictly to that theory without marring or disfiguring it by violences which form no part of it, by vain predictions which threaten with no certainty of fulfilment. The truth is that it is impossible to promise in advance to stick solely to either method—force or legality; and this is true for all parties. A Radical, M. Sigismund Lacroix, recognized this fact when he wrote some time ago: "Many people of whom I am one ... would hesitate to swear to stick, under all circumstances, to legal and peaceful means. This depends, not on opinions, but on situations. Revolutionary situations may arise, when to be a revolutionist will be a duty."[19]

Even admitting that there must be a revolution—a question which the events and not the wills of men will decide —this revolution, no matter what its incidents, will be only one term in the series of phenomena which are leading us from one social form to another, only one link in a chain, and is it reasonable, therefore, to hypnotize the laborers by concentrating their attention on that single link? What is necessary is to make socialists, to make the masses conscious of the economic movement in progress, to bring their wills into harmony with that movement, and thus to lead to the election of more and more socialists to our various elective assemblies, where it will be their duty and privilege to maintain the forgotten and despised rights of the people, and to effect, so far as they can, under the circumstances, the various ameliorations of the conditions and status of the toiling masses for which socialism is striving. The socialist party is the only party which pursues these aims in a practical fashion, by basing its tactics on the economic conditions of the environment. What is the use, therefore, of talking of anything but socialism, of expatiating on the nature of the crisis which will terminate the present phase of evolution and will be the beginning of a new phase? Why waste time talking about a contingent event that circumstances may force upon us in the future, but the time or character of which no man can define or describe to-day? At all events, if we must talk of revolution, our aim should be to overthrow the false ideas on this subject industriously circulated by our opponents with a view to deterring recruits from enlisting in the socialist army.

X [20]

Just as the idea of revolution is identified with the ideas of murder and destruction, in the same way the internationalism of the workers is identified with anti-patriotism. There is in the latter case as in the former a fundamental error, and it remains for me to show that, theoretically and practically, the identification of the internationalism of labor with anti-patriotism is unjustifiable. And, to begin with, he who says internationalism says internationalism, and does not say anti-nationalism; consequently, you see at once that no one ought—either to approve or condemn it—to use the word, internationalism, to express what it does not mean and what other words do mean.

Instead of allowing ourselves to be led astray by our various fantastic notions, let us here as elsewhere examine the facts and see what conclusions they impose upon us. Socialism flows from the facts, it follows them and does not precede them. This is the truth to which we must constantly return, which we must never forget. Now, the facts show us, *bon gré mal gré*, two things: on the one hand, the existence of countries (fatherlands); on the other, the existence, in every social stratum, of an international solidarity.

It is with countries as with classes; some deny the existence of the former, others of the latter. Now, in reason it is no more possible to deny the existence of the country (fatherland) than the existence of classes in that country. It is all right to look forward to the day when national patriotism shall be swallowed up in world-wide brotherhood, when classes shall vanish in human solidarity, but while waiting for the facts to turn this noble ideal into a reality, we must, in both cases, adapt ourselves to the facts as they actually are at present. To wish to suppress them (classes, etc.) does not suppress them, to protest against their existence does not at all prevent them from existing and, so long as countries and classes shall exist, it will be necessary for us, not to deny their existence in declamations in the Bryan-McKinley style, but to adapt our tactics to the facts which are the consequences of their existence.

Just as the feeling of national solidarity is added to the feeling of family solidarity, without destroying the latter, in the same way the relatively new sentiment of international solidarity is added to the former which is still retained. A new sentiment springing from a new situation does not annihilate the older sentiments and emotions as long as the conditions that gave them birth continue to exist, and families and nations are still in existence.

The tendency toward internationalism was inaugurated by capital. In obedience to its own law of continuous growth, it has, more and more, substituted international commerce for national trade. It has created industries whose raw materials come from abroad and whose products require, for an outlet, the universal or world market. It has thus developed the reciprocal interdependence of nations, no one of which to-day can live without the aid of the others.

Capitalist internationalism, moreover, pursues its ends with stern remorselessness. In order to lower national wages and gain greater profits, the capitalist does not hesitate to deprive his fellow-countrymen of work, and to import, to compete with them on the labor market, foreigners wonted by greater poverty to a lower standard of living, and therefore able and willing to work for lower wages. To prohibit them, not from employing foreigners, but from paying them less than the national rate of wages is the only effective means of meeting this evil. On the other hand, provided he sees a goodly profit in the transaction, the capitalist never hesitates to loan money or sell military supplies to a foreign country, though he thus increases its power to wage war against his own.

This international character, assumed by capital in all its forms, is, in its effects, co-extensive with the domain of human affairs. And so, as M. Aulard declared in a lecture about which there has been too much talk: "There are no national boundaries for reason and science. ... They are neither French, nor English, nor German, but international and human." How, therefore, can the workingmen be justly reproached for taking the road on which everything and everybody has started, and along which the capitalists have preceded them? Face to face with the international domination of capital, they have come to understand, in all civilized nations, the common character, the oneness, of their own interests. They are everywhere the victims of the same kind of exploitation, due everywhere to the same cause. The same facts have suggested to them the same demands, the same means and tactics to attain the same goal. International exploitation has thus given birth to an ever growing international solidarity among the workers who resist its encroachments. And the international concurrence of the workers is publicly declared by the world-wide celebration of the First day of May.

Notwithstanding the most sincere sentiment of international solidarity on both sides, the workingmen of two countries may still have to fight against each other. This is one of the numerous contradictions—and one of the most horrible—inherent in the capitalist regime, which is condemned to aspire to peace and to unchain the horrid dogs of war. While, for example, commerce on the world market requires peace, the bitterness of competition on that market begets conflicts.

* * *

To safeguard the little independence left to them as laborers, the workers have been led by the state of affairs, by actual conditions, as were the business men before them, to be internationalists; but they are patriots, and must be patriots only whenever their country—be it France or America—is menaced by danger from abroad.

I hope you now see that the internationalism of the workers and the socialists cannot, by any possibility lead to anti-patriotism. These are two distinct ideas which cannot be legitimately confounded, no matter what the object of this confusion. Our internationalism and our patriotism spring from two wholly distinct categories of facts, and different facts logically necessitate different solutions, logic consisting, here and everywhere, in adapting the solution to the facts and not in applying the same solution indiscriminately to all sorts of facts.

To sum up, workingmen and socialists ought to be internationalists in their relations with their toiling comrades when the interests of labor are at stake in times of peace, patriots and Frenchmen before all when France, our country shall be, if it must be, in danger of war, conscious always of the duty to be performed, conscious, if need be, especially in victory, of the duty of respecting in the case of others, especially the conquered, the rights that they claim for themselves.

* * *

I have finished. That is all that socialism means. I have taken pains to set it forth in its entirety, free from both the attenuations and the exaggerations by which it is often mutilated or disfigured, but which seem to me to have no foundation in reality. Its goal is the socialization of the means of labor which have already manifested collective tendencies—either in their mode of ownership or in the mode of their employment as exploiting agencies—and the abolition of classes. Its means, the transference to the political battlefield of the Class Struggle, the existence of which it is compelled to acknowledge. It must, for the time being, be resolved to preserve legality at home and peace abroad, but equally energetically determined to tolerate no measure that will make the situation of the toilers more intolerable, to preserve republican institutions intact and to defend the national territory against all foreign foes.

GABRIEL DEVILLE

Footnotes:

1. A word is needed to make the force of this sarcasm clear to American readers. There was formed around the late Benoît Malon, the founder of *La Revue Socialiste*, a small but very intelligent and influential school of socialists, who loved (and still

love) to prate about the inadequacy of Marxism, its neglect of various "factors," etc., etc. They regard Marxian economics as being true so far as they go, but as constituting a very inadequate and incomplete socialism, which it was reserved for them, by a beneficent Providence, to complete. Their own socialism they call "integral socialism." We have their like in America—men who use Marxian ammunition and belittle Marx.—Tr.

2. The French Webster.

3. "In fact the different classes dove-tail into each other, and there are always between two classes a multitude of unclassifiable hybrids, belonging wholly to neither class, in part to both."—Karl Kautsky.

4. In America where, since 1865, we have had no landed aristocracy, bourgeois and wealthy are well nigh synonymous.—Tr.

5. L'Evolution économique, p. 38.

6. This is not an English word, but I will take the liberty of borrowing it from the French.—Tr.

7. "The world owes every man a living," is a common saying.

8. M. Célestin Jonnart.

9. Déclaration du "Comité d'action de la gauche libérale."

10. Idem.

11. Committee of action of the Liberal Left.

12. March 8, 1893, 2d page.

13. "Political economy confuses on principle two very different kinds of private property, of which one rests on the producers' own labor, the other on the employment of the labor of others. It forgets that the latter not only is the direct antithesis of the former, but absolutely grows on its tomb only."—Marx, 1st vol. of *Capital*, Humboldt Edition, page 488.

14. M. Célestin Jonnart.

15. "In place of the old bourgeois society with its classes and class antagonisms we shall have an association in which the free development of each is the condition for the free development of all."—Marx and Engels, Communist Manifesto, page 43, New York, 1898, published by Nat. Ex. Committee of the Socialist Labor Party.

16. This word is used so exclusively in a technical sense by the Direct Legislation faddists, it may be necessary to say it is here used to denote originality and independent strength of mind, etc.—Tr.

17. "Industrial," as used here, and, indeed, correctly, it should be noted, does not include agricultural.—Tr.

18. Issue of Nov. 14, 1891.

19. *Le Radical*, May 30, 1893.

20. In France, where pseudo-patriotism, or jingoism, runs riot, the argument that international socialism is unpatriotic is much in vogue with the hireling scribes of capitalism. Hence, this section. In this country, owing in part to its geographical isolation, but still more to the almost complete lack of a sense of international solidarity on the part of the American worker, we seldom have to meet this argument, and so I will condense and abridge this section.—Tr.

The State and Socialism

I

What do the socialists think about the State? How do they regard it theoretically in the present and for the future? What are the practical consequences which result from their views? Such are the questions which I propose to answer here and now, and this answer will be the one which appears to me to be in the most perfect harmony with the facts, for conformity to the facts is, and ever must be, the guiding principle of modern scientific socialism, of our socialism.

What is the State?

Here I could easily make a show of learning by quoting a number of definitions drawn from philosophers and writers more or less famous; but such an enumeration would occupy space and time without being of any real advantage to us; for, in most cases, the word State is identified with other words such as society, nation or government, and so these confused definitions would not be helpful to my hearers or readers as the authors of the definitions did not themselves comprehend the essential distinctions. Do not fancy that this criticism is made by the socialists alone. You will find this same confusion set forth in the work of one of our adversaries, in *La Politique* of M. Charles Benoist,[1] who is the last, as far as I know, who has treated these questions among us.

And so, partly because he is the most recent writer, and has thus been able to profit by the labors of all the others, but more particularly because he has succeeded in avoiding confusions of a nature to obscure the question at issue, from among all the definitions that bourgeois writers have given of the State, I select for the purposes of my discussion that of M. Charles Benoist.

"The State," he maintains, "is the moral personification

of the nation endowed with perpetuity and incarnated in institutions, clothed with the power and right of constraint. It may be recognized by these two signs: it makes laws and it levies taxes." [2]

The State, I will maintain in my turn, is the public power of coercion, created and maintained in human societies by their division into classes, and which, having force at its disposal, makes laws and levies taxes.

The only real difference between these two definitions – but it is a difference of the first importance – consists in the fact that in the latter – *i.e.* for socialists – the existence of the State in a society is bound up with the existence of classes in that society. Hence, this conclusion: before classes came into being there was no State; when classes shall cease to exist there will be no State. While in the former, – *i. e.* for bourgeois theorists, – the State exists independently of every other social institution and, in particular, of classes. According to M. Charles Benoist, "it is congenital in human societies, and they could not live without it." [3] Contrary to our opinion, the same author thinks that "primitive communities, the embryos of society; contain an embryonic State," [4] and that the State is a "moral personality endowed with perpetuity." [5]

Parenthetically, we remark here again that passion for perpetuity so marked in the ruling, property-holding class and in the economists, their official defenders. According to them, indeed, the situation from which the capitalist profits is simply the realization, the embodiment of eternal verities, and eternal capital must go on eternally breeding more capital. The capitalists, in their insatiable thirst for gain, cry to their God with all zeal and sincerity: "As it was in the beginning, is now, and ever shall be: world without end. Amen"; but this prayer, even though it be granted, is not enough. They require, besides this, the protection of the State. And so they and their theorists have eagerly and emphatically pronounced themselves in favor of its perpetuity, blaming its intervention only when its powers are not exerted in their behalf.

Which of the two – the socialist theory of the State or the bourgeois theory -corresponds the more closely to the reality? I believe that I can prove – at all events, I am going to try to prove – that it is ours. From the definition that I have given of the State, it follows in the first place that the State has not always existed, that there have been societies without a State, but the absence of a State did not prevent these societies from having an organization. My thesis is that a social organization is possible without a State, and that the State appears and subsists only in societies divided into classes.

Some societies without States have continued to exist down to our own times among the Indians of North America. And it was by studying the social regime of these Indians, and of the Iroquois especially, that Morgan was able, by his remarkable work, *Ancient Society,* to enable us at last to clearly understand the primitive societies of Greece and Italy, societies which were based, like the Indian societies, upon the *gens.* [6]

Morgan's work has not been translated into French, but it has been epitomized and perfected by Engels, [7] and the historical details that follow are drawn from this study of Engels.

What was the organization established among the Indians of America, and notably among the Iroquois, *i. e.* among those of the Indians who developed their social forms the most highly? Its foundation was the *gens,* just as it was among all the barbarians whose mode of life we have been able to ascertain. At this point it suffices for us to know that the *gens* was a particular grouping of individuals, having a real or assumed common origin, dwelling in the same region, and never marrying members of the same *gens.*

All the members of the Indian *gens* were free and equal, and acted as brothers toward one another. In time of peace they elected a sachem, whose election they could always annul at their pleasure, and whose authority, destitute of any means of coercion, was simply moral. As to the chiefs chosen in case of war, they were charged only with the conduct of expeditions and their appointments, like those of the sachems, were revocable. Sovereignty belonged to the assembly of adults, men and women.

In the tribe, a coalition of a certain number of *gentes,* and in the federation of tribes which was the most highly developed social form of the Indians, the sovereign power was exercised by a coalition of sachems forming either the tribal council, or the federal council, and their deliberations took place in the presence of the members of the tribe or of the federation, who had the right to participate in the discussion. But, the sachems composing these councils could at any moment be recalled by their respective *gentes.* Moreover, in the tribal council all the sachems, and in the federal council, where the vote was by tribes, all the tribes had to agree to render a decision valid.

Therefore, if we find here a social organization, we find nothing corresponding to the State, not only as I have defined it, but even as our adversaries define it. For we do not find here the slightest trace of that which constitutes the State according to M. Chas. Benoist – no authority "clothed with force and the right of constraint," and the law, the guiding rule of a certain collectivity, is merely the effective expression of the will of that collectivity, and there are no taxes.

To prove the truth of my thesis – the existence of societies without States – I have referred you to specific facts. To support his – the existence of the State from the origin of societies – M. Charles Benoist contents himself with affirming that "the first military chief was the first State." [8] Now, if it is true that the executive power has most frequently sprung from the institution of a supreme military command, it is false that the military chief has always had any special power whatsoever apart from the direction of the operations of war. In particular, it is false that he was "the guardian of order" [9] in collectivities based on the *gens.*

Order in these communities – as has been proved in the case of the American Indians – was admirably maintained spontaneously without any system or apparatus of coercion, notwithstanding the number of common affairs to be adjusted, because their institutions did, not give rise to any antagonism between categories of individuals, for all were free and equal. And we know what fine men these Indians were, how noble their moral qualities – save where their enemies were concerned – their energy and their dignity.

I must here forestall an interpretation, which the adversaries of socialism often give to our arguments, and point out that the eulogy in certain respects of primitive societies does not at all imply a purpose to revert to the ancient social forms. Let these gentlemen, so hostile to socialism and so proud of their civilization, calm themselves. We do not dream of leading them back to that which they call the state of Nature. It would, indeed, be too great a change for most of them to have to substitute the uprightness and horror of falsehood of the Indian for their dishonest polemical methods.

If I have spoken at such length of the Indians of North America, it is because it has been possible in our day to study among them social forms which have elsewhere disappeared centuries since, and in that way to demonstrate the existence of organized societies without a State. Now, just as the phases of evolution – infancy, youth, mature age, old age – with their special characteristics, follow each other in much the same way in all men whose development is not arrested by special circumstances, in the same way the various human societies – from the point of view of the family, property, religion and politics – pass through analogous phases and, like individuals, make more or less progress along the path of evolution common to them all. And, while, as Marx said, "the country that is more developed industrially only shows, to the less developed, the image of its own future," [10] in their turn the more backward countries present to the others the image of their own past. As a matter of fact, in all peoples whose early institutions it has been possible to study, the *gens* has been found to have been, at a certain stage of development, the social unit.

Notably the *gens* existed in Greece and at Rome, and, back of the Greek *gens* and the Roman *gens,* such as they are known to us, glimpses may be caught, though they disappeared long before, of the characteristic features of the Indian *gens.* Thus in the Homeric era, where, however, the *gens* was already modified and where the elements of a new organization were making their appearance, we find still subsisting the sovereignty of the popular assembly and the non-existence of a public power distinct from the assemblage of the adult males and capable of being turned against them. If, on the other hand, we see there the dawn of the establishment of noble families and the appearance in the germ of the principle of heredity in the selection of the military chief, it is obvious, nevertheless, that the chief, the *basileus,* has only military, religious and judicial attributes. A political or governmental power, analogous to that which essentially constitutes the State, does not yet exist.

How did the transformation take place? How was the State born?

The distinctive mark of the social organization based on the *gens* is the solidarity of the interests of all its members. Between them there are no antagonistic situations, and therefore no desire for the repression of some and no power of coercion for the benefit of others. The offspring of social conditions of an extreme simplicity, this organization could not adapt itself to more complex conditions of life. At the best era of the *gens,* production was very limited and the means of existence depended chiefly on the clemency or rigor of the climate. But while what we call the New World (America) was, before the European conquest, very nearly without any animals suited for domestication, the Old World was abundantly supplied with them. And it seems that this is what enabled it to surpass so prodigiously and so comparatively quickly the inferior degree of culture at which the Indians of America stopped short.

The domestication of animals, their breeding, the formation of large herds, and later on new discoveries like those of iron and its utilization in tilling the ground, together with the development of various handicrafts, systematized and increased production, compared to its former condition, to such an extent that men were able to produce in excess of their needs. Slavery became possible as soon as a greater number of laborers were required by the social conditions realized, and thereafter they made slaves of the prisoners of war whom the Indians either killed or adopted into the *gens*.

While there was thus created the division between free men and slaves, the free men themselves were divided into rich and poor.

Instead of remaining the common property of the tribe or of the *gens*, the herds soon became the individual property of the heads of families. This property in flocks and herds had the peculiarity of increasing in the hands of its holders. The importance of private property and of the principal proprietors increased, and the principle or mode of private appropriation was at last extended so as to include the land. The inequality of wealth, which was the consequence of these facts, created the germ of an aristocracy.

Wealth being from that time the object to strive for, war upon neighboring peoples, solely with a view to pillage and booty, became a permanent fact. The authority of the military chiefs, and especially of the supreme chief, increased. The choice of their successors from among their next of kin – made freely at first by preference – became a regular custom and finally the accepted rule. There was thus formed a category of families, already powerful through their wealth, to whom belonged the more important functions. Then, there were on the one side a minority enjoying hereditary privileges, and on the other side the non-privileged and the slaves. There you have a society divided into antagonistic classes – a servitude, a subordination existing which make a power of domination within the society indispensable, while. subjection and domination were unknown and unnecessary in the social organization based on the *gens*.

For the security of a social order involving the division of the population into classes, a public power calculated to compel the respect of the non-privileged is necessary. "Arm a man," Stendhal said ironically, "and then continue to oppress him, and you will see that he will be perverse enough, if he can, to turn his arms against you." [11] The privileged at once suspect this latent perversity. And so as soon as a population is split up into classes, the armed force no longer corresponds to the whole of the male population able to wield arms, and the constituted force can be opposed to the rest of the population. Besides the armed force, the public power, necessary for every society based on the separation of men into classes, includes various means of coercion, such as prisons, etc., that were not to be found in societies built upon the *gens*.

To provide for the support of this public power resources are needed, and this accounts for the appearance of taxes.

We now see how there grew up, along with the influence – at the least predominant – of the aristocracy in the general administration and passing of laws, the repressive and fiscal institutions which, as we have seen, characterize the State.

Thus the State whose non-existence in a society may be demonstrated so long as there are no classes in that society, makes its appearance in a more or less developed form with the existence of classes and the antagonism they involve. The product of a definite social order, it will last as long as the circumstances that have rendered it inevitable.

II

Undoubtedly the disappearance of primitive communities, of societies based on the *gens,* was a true progress, and yet they produced – as I have just pointed out in the case of the Indians of America – men endued, in general, with a moral superiority which the succeeding social organizations have been unable to attain in a like degree. Here, it seems, there is a contradiction which, as it requires some explanatory comments, leads me to say a word on a question raised before you by our eminent friend Jaurès. I do not pretend that there is any absolute urgency to enter upon this question. here; but I hope you will excuse the digression.

In our opinion, he has asked us[12], is there progress in the march of human development, and, if there is progress, what is its cause? For his part, he finds the required explanation in a predisposition of the human mind to aspire toward the realization of righteousness. Obviously there has been progress. But it is not through aspiration toward the realization of righteousness that this progress has been accomplished. Although men had from the beginning a more or less confused sentiment of justice, progress has been brought about neither by this sentiment nor by the idealist manifestations of the human conscience; and the propositions, which the subject I am discussing to-day have led me to establish, furnish the proof of this.

The extension of private property, as well as the disappearance of the *gens,* which finally resulted from it constituted, as I have said, an historical progress; but, so far as concerns human dignity and morality, the extension of the one and the disappearance of the other, far from constituting a progress, have resulted in a manifest degeneration. The most despicable sentiments then made their appearance. Greed, hypocrisy and false-speaking, induced by personal interests over-excited at the expense of the primitive solidarity, presided over the ruin of the old organization and the appearance of

67

classes.

From that moment to this, every step forward in the conquest of new productive powers by the genius of man, has been the source of misfortunes for the exploited masses. That which has been a progress from the point of view of the evolution of human intelligence, that which in itself should have been a good, has too often, from the point of view of its immediate effect upon men, been in fact a good for a minority only, and an evil, a source of sufferings for all others. This contradiction, this conversion of blessings into curses, which springs from the exploitation of the majority, is, so long as classes exist, the foundation of the social order, and it will last as long as classes and the exploitation that they imply shall exist. And the dominant idea, if it is necessary to specify one in particular, has been the striving after individual enrichment rather than the tendency toward a more perfect justice.

Yes, there has been progress. Its measure is the degree of knowledge attained; its cause is the mental activity of men exerting itself on the materials provided by the external environment, and developing in proportion to its exertion and to the increase in number and complexity of the materials at its disposition. [13]

It would be impossible to attribute a finer role to human intelligence, since man has thus been his own creator. For, by elaborating at any given moment the materials offered him by the external environment, he adds to those materials and in this way makes possible for the better trained, better equipped brain of the future a new and more perfect elaboration. The brain has the faculty of working up the elements drawn from the environment, just as the digestive apparatus has the faculty of digesting. But the power of elaborating and the power of digesting do not necessarily imply elaboration and digestion. In order for the latter to take place, there is requisite something external to man, something more or less substantial, having objective reality, which man only assimilates more or less thoroughly and transforms.

The nature of man being given, his action is above all dependent upon the special character of the external environment in which he lives. He can act upon this environment, transform it and increase its resources and thereby act upon those who shall come after him and who will have as their determining environment the new environment which he will have aided in creating. Yet, though he is able thus to modify the environment by which he has been formed, he not only can, of course, have no retrospective effect upon the conditions of which he is himself the product and must simply take the elements of his environment exactly as they are transmitted to him, but besides this, whatever maybe the special intentions and purposes that govern his action, the latter leads to unforeseen results. Just as he cannot choose his starting-point, so he cannot control the ultimate result of his innovations. [14]

The inventions and not the intentions of men have been the cause of progress. If, in particular, the intention to achieve more perfect justice – which could not have been the motive of many of those whose labors have brought progress to pass – had embodied itself in facts with the advance of progress, those whose situation is such that they must necessarily benefit by every increase of justice, the exploited, ought to have seen the degree of their exploitation gradually falling lower and lower. Now, it is just the contrary that is proven for each of the great periods of history. To take the situation of the exploited masses during the period of the wages-system as an example, things, far from going from better to better, have gone from bad to worse.

This will not be doubted by those who do not limit themselves to comparing absurdly the mode of life of the laborer of to-day with the mode of life of the laborer of former times. It is ridiculous to draw an argument from a comparison of the life of the working-class only at two different periods – one in which the non-satisfaction of wants is due to the fact that the wants themselves are unknown and unfelt, and the other in which the same wants have been acquired and cannot be satisfied. What should be compared in order to estimate exactly the change for the better or the worse are the respective economic positions of the capitalists and the wage-workers at the two periods. At all events, it cannot be denied by those who have – and I am of the number – the smallest possible tendency to make themselves the apologists of the past, that the wages of the man sufficed in former times for the support of the whole family, and that to-day there must be added to those wages those of the wife and the child to enable the family to live no better relatively to the conditions of life normal now and then.

The result of progress has been to increase the knowledge and power of man, to multiply the forces at his service and to extend the possibility of more comfortable living and fuller development. The *possibility* of greater comfort, I said, but, alas, the realization of this comfort is possible only to a minority, and for the majority it is too often but a source of new suffering. Such is the contradictory result of progress. And from the dawn of civilization, from the time when classes and with them the rudiments of this new institution, the State, began to exist, down to the present hour when classes still persist, human development has been unable to escape from this contradiction.

It is certain that if we judge this development in its entirety, from the point of view of the more elevated conception of justice made possible, suggested at the present day by a disinterested observation of the material possibilities, we cannot fail to find that the facts, no longer weighed by the results that they have had to the injury of certain categories of persons, but taken in the mass and considered in themselves, are more nearly in harmony with this conception as we approach more nearly the time when this conception shall be able to impose itself upon humanity, and if this were not so it would be a cause for surprise.

But it is also certain that, under the regime of classes,

civilization inexorably implies the exploitation of certain classes by others and that, therefore, the progress accomplished, especially in the mode of production, instead of being immediately beneficial to all, is an assured benefit to a minority only, and is often an immediate ill for many – for all those notably whose former means of existence are destroyed without compensation by a technical improvement. The latter, the exploited, under the blow of this new evil, struggle to rid themselves of it. Frequently, not grasping the cause of this but too real evil, they attribute it to a scientific discovery, to a machine for instance, instead of putting the blame where it belongs, upon the mode of appropriation of the results of science. This conflict more or less ably waged, which would not exist if the conditions of life for all classes were constantly improving, justifies the words of Marx: "It is the bad side (of human nature) which produces the movement that makes history, by engendering conflict." [15]

This conflict is precisely – and here I return to the true subject of this lecture – the efficient reason for the persistence of the State.

III

As soon as there are in a society a possessing class and a dispossessed class, there exists in that society a constant source of collisions which the social organization would not long resist, if there was not a power charged with maintaining, to use the consecrated phrase, the "established order," charged, in other words, with the protection of the economic situation of the possessing party, and therefore with the duty of ensuring the submission of the dispossessed party. Now, from its very birth, this has been the role of the State.

An organ of conservation, the offspring of struggles or threats of struggles between conflicting interests, conflicting because of the antagonism of material conditions, born – as we have seen – with the division of society into classes, the State has evolved with the development of that division, *i. e.,* in short, with the economic relations which form the basis of that division; but, under the various appearances it has worn, its object has remained the same because, ever since the appearance of classes, it has always had a privileged economic situation to defend and conflicts to repress. When it is known that the State is a class-instrument it is easy to understand whence comes its character of relative permanence which bourgeois writers point out without explaining.

Thus M. Charles Benoist writes: "In the notion of the State the moderns have introduced a new element – permanence." [16] Why have the moderns "introduced" this new element? Was it theirs to choose whether to introduce it or not? These are the questions to which in M. Benoist you will find no response. M. Charles Benoist, I repeat, shows that it is there; he does not explain it. "The French State," he continues, "is the same under this third Republic as under Napoleon I, under Louis XI, under Henry IV and under Charles V. It is true the government changes its form by revolutions, and its personnel by the mere lapse of time, but the government is not the State; it is only the envelope and, as it were, the clothing of the State[17] ... it changes, while the State does not change. One of the chief traits of the State, perpetuity, or at least long duration, government does not have[18] ... Government is that which passes away in the State which abides. Governments, indeed, are like the hours, the successive periods, the phases of the evolution of the State." [19]

Here we have affirmations exact in substance, if not always in form. Yet, in my judgment, they are comprehensible only to those who know what it is that is permanent in the State and the reason of that permanence, only to those who know, to put it differently, that the State is, under its varying forms, a class-instrument which has lasted and will last on that account so long as there have been and so long as there shall be classes.

He who understands and admits this, will readily and

clearly see, I do not say, and I beg that no one will represent me as saying, the uselessness of changes in governmental forms or constitutions, but the naiveté of expecting from these changes results that it is impossible for them to give. It is now possible to gauge the candor of our inflexible radicals who attach so much importance to pure questions of form and proclaim such a strong intellectual antipathy for our collectivist theory, although they can view with complacency the farcical middle-class attempts to make the State the impartial protector of capital and labor alike.

I have pointed out to you the genesis of the State and shown you its necessary, inevitable character. I have striven, in a word, to justify the terms of the definition given in the first part of this lecture. Whether or not I have succeeded in my task, you must at least have been convinced that the socialist definitions are not arbitrary. Our opponents may very legitimately discuss them and attempt to prove that our terminology is wrong. That which they have no right to do is to attack socialism without taking the pains to know clearly and definitely the meaning that, rightly or wrongly, it gives to the words that it employs. By disdaining this elementary precaution, they expose themselves to the most ridiculous confusion and waste their time in combatting something quite different from that which the socialists defend.

This has happened in the case of capital. In order to understand what we mean by the suppression of capital, one must know that capital is for us a character which the means of production have taken on under given, definite social conditions, and which they may lose without affecting their existence in the slightest. It is just the same in the case of the wage-system and wages. The latter term cannot, according to us, be applied to any system of remuneration whatsoever, but only to a mode of remuneration presupposing surplus-labor. It is just the same finally in the case of the word State, which means, in our opinion, a system of social organization which implies necessarily the division of society into classes.

73

It is not by caprice – it seems to me that I have furnished you the proof of this in the case of the State – that socialists give such or such a meaning to such or such a word. Of course, they may be mistaken; but one can reasonably criticize their theories only by using words in the same sense that they do.

At bottom I am not far from thinking that this ignorance of our definitions is wilful ignorance. It must be more easy to refute that which we do not say and which they put in our mouths, than that which we do say and which they ignore. There are some ideas incompatible with the tranquil security of the possessing class, the class controlling production and power. Among these ideas, the ideas of surplus labor and of the existence of distinct classes are particularly repugnant to those who profit by just those conditions. They feel that the mere divulgation of the secret of their power is an impairment of that power, and the very truth contained in our definitions appears to them a danger. And so, not content with avoiding this truth in their own definitions, they avoid it – so far as they are able to – in ours. In order to confound us the more triumphantly, they first change the meaning of our words, then, after the words, they travesty our ideas, and then they have no trouble to demonstrate the absurdity of he fabrications they attribute to us.

We know what the State is. The State, for us socialists, is not any social organization whatsoever. It is, I have said, and I believe I afterward justified the terms of this definition, the public power of coercion created and maintained in human societies by their division into classes, and which, having force at its disposal, makes laws and levies taxes. What should be the attitude of socialists toward the State? This is the question that I am now going to examine and that is easy to answer if we bear in mind that the State, having been created by the division of society into classes, is inevitably maintained by that division.

As soon as it is understood that the State is not an independent organism, having its own existence without regard to the interlaced economic relations of men, but is necessarily subordinate to the division of society into classes, and, in consequence, to a particular economic situation, no party whatever can reasonably set up, as the immediate goal for its efforts, the abolition of the State, nor the suppression of the political power that constitutes it. The State, being a consequence, cannot disappearance before the disappearance of the social conditions of which it is the necessary result.

Since the disappearance of the State implies the previous modification of the social conditions, of the economic relations, ought the attack to be made directly upon these relations? Let us revert to the conclusions already established: a certain economic situation begot classes; as soon as there were in the population privileged orders, the latter needed means to preserve their point of vantage, to impose upon all respect for their privileges, and hence the State was born. Hence, the economic situation to be transformed, the situation which begets classes, has its guarantee of perpetuity in the State. That is, in other words, it cannot be radically effected, in a general way, so long as the State shall defend it against the direct attacks that may be made upon it.

In short, one can abolish the State only after having suppressed classes, and one cannot modify the economic relations of which classes are merely the personification, without acting first upon the State. The question formulated just above is solved. It is necessary to act upon the State and not to aim at present at its abolition; to act upon the State because this is the only way in which it is possible to so adjust the conditions and relations of persons as to bring them into harmony with the economic evolution in progress and thus to make possible the suppression of classes; not to aim at present at its abolition, because it cannot be abolished before the disappearance of classes, a disappearance that it must itself help to bring to pass. The only practical line of conduct for socialists, for workingmen, is, to use the customary expression, the conquest of political power, the conquest of the State. It is the more and more complete control by them of the public powers, that all their efforts must have in view; it is to this object that all their tactics must be devoted.

The struggle of classes with each other has an economic object, but the form of this struggle must necessarily be political; for, between the material position to be ameliorated and the accomplished amelioration, there rises up like a barrier the power of the State which alone, whatever class controls it, can give a general and mandatory character to the results of the struggle. The State makes the law, and it is only by placing oneself on the political ground that one can succeed in participating in the making of law. History and reason agree in proving the truth of this thesis: the struggle of the "lower" classes is really effective only when it assumes a political character.

Not to speak of the past, what do we see, in fact, in the different countries round about us where there have, notwithstanding, long had, less restricted than us, the possibility of conducting the struggle on the economic ground? In the countries still without universal suffrage, the struggle has been or is to obtain it. In the countries where universal suffrage is in operation, however imperfect the system may be, the masses are soon driven, by the results of relative successes, to apply themselves principally to returning more and more socialists to the various elective assemblies. Undeniably, without being a partisan of all or nothing, one does not obtain immediately as much as one could wish, but by what other process could one do better? Much of the success on the economic ground, indeed, is due to the aid of socialists in office, due, in other words, to political action.

Socialists must work for the continuation of this regular movement by which socialist men and ideas penetrate more and more the elective bodies, and this implies a constant propaganda among the masses, It is true that circumstances, paying no heed to our will, may impose upon us later on another mode of action, but that is a matter with which we have nothing to do at present. So long as such circumstances have not come to pass, socialism has nothing to gain by departing from legality, and, in any case, it has nothing to gain by manifesting itself under the form of riots or disturbances. I have explained my views on this subject in a former lecture. [20] I will not repeat myself here, but confine myself to showing that the only present task of socialists must be, to swell the ranks of the socialists, both voters and officials.

The great argument against these tactics is the reproach of parliamentarism[21] flung at their partisans; as if one was responsible for the bad sides of parliamentarism, because, while parliamentarism exists, one makes use of it! As if conformity to a law or submission to an institution involved their approbation!

It is easy to criticize parliamentarism and to criticize it justly, but criticism does not prevent it from existing. Modify the machinery of parliamentarism if you can just as much as you may be able to, and I can see no objection, but rather the contrary. Nevertheless it is to be feared that those who are unwilling to deceive themselves about the modifications at present possible, will soon see that it would be just as easy to accomplish at once the substitution of the socialist society for the capitalist society as to secure, under the capitalist regime, any radical changes in parliamentarism. Is it worth while, then, to undertake special campaigns to secure improvements which, however valuable they would be in another environment, are none the less at present either impracticable or of secondary importance?

To seek to accomplish a thorough-going reform of parliamentarism in an environment in which parliamentarism is the governmental form of the capitalist society is equivalent to aiming immediately and before all else at the abolition of the State, and we have seen what must be thought of that aspiration. If we take advantage of all favorable opportunities to effect all possible reforms and improvements in the working of the parliamentary or representative system, we will do well, provided that we do not allow ourselves to be turned aside from the real object of our endeavors, viz., the more and more complete conquest of the political power to be used to give effect to the economic demands of the workers.

Those who strive to keep the workingmen out of the field of political action do not suspect, of course, that they are thus playing the game of the ruling class. By shouting, "No politics!" they are merely echoing the rallying cry that the bourgeoisie has always given to the working-class. The property qualification for the suffrage and the absence of remuneration for office-holders, such as members of the English Parliament, have been nothing but means to keep workingmen out of politics. These means are no longer efficacious. Are those who call themselves socialists ambitious to accomplish, for the profit of the bourgeoisie, what they, by themselves, have finally failed to effect?

In the presence of living issues, the socialists of to-day can no longer confine themselves to academic discussion. The necessity of formulating practical, incontrovertible conclusions forces itself upon them, so that I must enter upon the examination of certain tactics much urged at this time in opposition to those, the correctness of which, I believe, I have just demonstrated.

IV [22]

To compel the capitulation of the capitalist society and its organic protector, the State, some socialists have recently imagined that the political struggle was insufficient and that the recourse must be had to the "general strike." Let us talk of the general strike.

I begin by declaring that I will make no attempt to solve the question as to whether there ought or ought not to be strikes. The question cannot present itself in this way. The strike is the inevitable product of an economic environment based on antagonistic interests and, even though it should wish to, socialism could not suppress the strike, any more than it can, at once, suppress the State or the capitalist society. The only weapon of the working-class on the economic ground, the; only means of defense or attack which it has for the protection of its immediate material interests, the strike is a right which the workingmen are right in jealously guarding. But if socialists should use every effort to maintain intact this right for the workers, for all the workers, it is not their business to incite them to make use of it. It is not for them either to provoke or inhibit strikes. It is for those immediately interested, those who will have to endure the consequences of their decision, to decide, without pressure of any kind from the non-interested. When those whose interests are at stake have pronounced themselves in favor of a strike, we ought to aid them to gain every possible advantage from the situation in which they have placed themselves. That is, generally speaking, what is and what should be the conduct of socialists so far as concerns strikes.

Having posited this so as to forestall, so far as possible, all false interpretations, I will add that the strike is a weapon, the effectiveness of which we should be careful not to exaggerate, no matter what our point of view may be. Under the most favorable circumstances it may have been able to compel some employers to yield; it has never been able to produce the slightest radical change in the employing system. To look at it more in detail, there have been numerous strikes, great resistance-funds have been amassed and spent, countless efforts and dollars have been expended, and what has been the result attained? Here or there, there have obtained some ameliorations; but even where these ameliorations have not been merely ephemeral, they have not been incompatible with the increasing prosperity of capital.

The strike is no longer a means on the general efficacy of which one can still cherish illusions. It has passed long since from theory into practice. We have seen, in the United States and. England chiefly, tremendous strikes disposing of enormous resources, prepared and carried on with an incomparable talent for organization, and to what have they led? In the United States socialism is indisputably much more backward than in Europe. In England, where the strike was formerly lauded as a panacea, they have come to understand its dangers and defects so thoroughly that, on the whole, hostility to it is becoming more and more general, and political action is growing in favor at its expense.

The experiment has been tried. On the economic ground, the struggle is too unequal for the working-class. However great its sacrifices, its self-denial and its energy, it loses the battle more often than it wins it, and when it does win it, the advantages that it reaps do not alter the fact that the victory is very expensive and precarious. On the political ground, on the contrary, the laborer can not only meet the capitalist on a footing of equality, but, as the working-class is more numerous than the bourgeois class, it enjoys a real advantage; so that on the political ground it is for socialism a mere matter of propaganda and time. Do you honestly believe that we would not be far nearer our goal to-day if there had been devoted to the political struggle half, and only half, of the efforts and money that have been expended on strikes that have failed?

Under these conditions, a socialist faction wishes to generalize the strike – a weapon good, at the most, only in particular cases – and to set the general strike before the proletariat as their goal.

If I have made my meaning clear, by reason of the simple fact that it is an economic struggle, that it diverts, in part, if not altogether, the workingman from the political struggle which is the true struggle for him to engage and persevere in, the general strike should be immediately rejected by all minds conscious of the facts and their consequences, by all those who reason without prejudice and "do not pay themselves with words." [23]

Moreover, even though one were to disregard this consideration, the system of the general strike would not bear scrutiny. We have shown the impotence of the strike as a means of emancipation. To generalize the strike – conceding the possibility of this -would not reduce this impotence, but rather the contrary.

The difficulties, springing from an organization and resources which have scarcely ever – as perfect and large as they have been – been equal to the requirements, would be, by the very extent of the strike, largely increased. The dangers springing from exasperation, always possible and actually but too pardonable, would increase in their turn with the growth of the numbers involved in the strike. Who can guarantee that all the strikers would preserve their calm self-restraint in the face of the measures habitually taken in such cases by all governments and which would in this case necessarily be aggravated – displays of military power, provocations by the police, arrests, condemnations, brutalities and injustices of every kind? Who can guarantee that the blow of a stone or a club, thrown by a striker in a very comprehensible access of wrath would not be the signal for a new massacre of the workers?

But even if all these dangers and difficulties were avoided or overcome, the proletarian movement would inevitably be overwhelmed. The partisans of the general strike have not, I suppose, the assurance to count on success at the first attempt. They must necessarily, however confident they may be in their ultimate success, face the eventuality of a check: on any ground to say struggle implies saying possibility of defeat. But, while, on the political ground, a check, for from depressing courage, tends rather to stimulate it, a defeat on the economic ground is disastrous. The facts are there to prove that a conquered strike has resulted, in various places, in a diminution of the number of militant proletarians.

In a political check, one's pride or vanity is wounded;

81

one is vexed, I will not say at being beaten, for it may chance in this matter for one to be very emphatically beaten and yet satisfied, but at the insufficiency of the result attained; one wishes for revenge and one works for it with enthusiasm. In the economic check, in the failure of a strike, one is a victim of real sufferings; there is added to the material sufferings of the conquered striker the moral suffering of seeing his loved family and comrades suffer bootlessly; discouraged and disconsolate, he vows not to renew the conflict in order that he may never again witness such a spectacle, and he withdraws from the movement. This effect would be produced far more powerfully by a check or failure of a general strike, as the attempt would have given birth to greater hopes; this would be a terrible blow for the socialist party – a blow that would greatly retard its progress. [24]

V

I believe I have shown the impotence of the strike in general and of the general strike in particular as a substitute for political action for the emancipation of the proletariat. Considering it then as proven that the first task and duty of the latter is the conquest of the public powers, let us see what should be the attitude of the socialists in the various elective bodies.

They must always undertake the defense of the disinherited in our social environment, not only take a hand in all reforms of all kinds, but agitate for and bring into effect as soon as possible, by adapting themselves to circumstances, every measure calculated to afford immediate relief to the working-class, to the wage-slaves, to all the exploited of the capitalist regime, by restricting their exploitation. We have never been of the number of those who say: "All or nothing!" and still less of those who say: "From bad to worse!" [25] We always accept everything which leads us from bad to better, merely insisting upon not halting along the road but upon continuing to go forward from better to better aiming at the well-being of all, conformably to the economic conditions which render its attainment finally possible. To do each moment everything of this kind that is feasible, without ever losing sight of our goal – that is what ought to be the rule of conduct of socialists elected to office.

Ought they in addition to this general tendency to have, as some maintain, a particular tendency to advance deliberately toward the absorption by the present State of the various branches of industry? In my opinion the question ought not to be asked in this categorical fashion, as one's opinion on the advantages of increasing the number and bulk of the public services in the capitalist environment must vary with the varying circumstances.

Yes, the conversion of such or such branches of industry into public services directly dependent upon the State, may be a good thing in one case and a bad thing in another. It all depends, in fact, among us, on the character of the majority that makes the law. An additional public service being that much additional power for the State, we must strengthen the positions which are more or less in our own hands and not those which are in the hands of our enemies. Let us first effect our entrance into the place; we will strengthen it afterward. You see, all roads lead us to the same inevitable conclusion: the first thing to do is to effect our entrance in larger and larger numbers into the elective assemblies. For what I have said about the State is equally applicable, though in a less degree, to the departments and the municipalities – in a less degree because not only is the sphere of action smaller but especially because the power is less, and it is this which gives their signal importance to legislative elections.

Though socialism succeeds in extending the public services when it is to its advantage to do so, or in exacting various social reforms, this does not constitute State socialism, [26 it is simply a more or less complete infiltration of socialism into the State. Socialists, in fact, do not expect to accomplish serious reforms while the State is wholly in the hands of their opponents. They expect to do this only after the State shall be more or less fully in their own hands, Pure socialism tends to bring the social means of production under the control of society, which is not an organism severed from the individuals composing it any more than the individuals are not conceivable apart from it, and whose enlarged action, wholly intentional and voluntary, is the very condition of a more ample, a more real liberty of all the individuals. Statism tends to turn everything over to the State which is a body apart from individuals and above them. The distinction has, it must be confessed, no great practical interest in France at present, because we have universal suffrage and the Republic and therefore the State is independent of the masses of the nation only on account of the ignorance of those masses. Let this ignorance be dissipated – and this is the tendency of the socialist propaganda – and the mass of the nation will have a direct influence on the State, which means that they will use the State as a means of action, and it is for this that they must make the conquest of the State. To understand this is to be able to do it.

This is not the case everywhere, because everywhere the political evolution has not progressed so far as it has in France. In places where it is otherwise, for example in Germany, where the State is independent of the nation, and where socialism is powerful, there has developed a certain doctrine under the name of State socialism and, there, this distinction, which has no great interest among us, is very important, all the more because State socialism has been conceived precisely in order to supply the State with a means of combatting pure socialism which is the only socialism, and to arrest its expansion.

This "dike" has never been very effective, moreover, according to M. Léon Say, who, making, as do all those conversant with the subject, the distinction I have just made, said in an address at Amiens: "The State socialism of Prince Bismarck and of the German professors commonly known as the economists (socialists) of the chair, has not impaired the force of the socialist current; it has, on the contrary, rendered it more formidable, and the bureaucratic dike with which it was intended to block its progress may well be swept away some fine day, in spite of the pains taken and the scientific precautions used in building it." [27] Therefore, let us not confound State socialism with the infiltration of socialism into the State, and let us endeavor to increase this infiltration as much as possible until socialism shall be mistress of the State. That day will be, not the last day of the State, but the first day of the last phase of its evolution.

The disappearance of the State, as I have said, implies the disappearance of classes, *i.e.,* the previous modification of social conditions. This modification must be brought about by law, and it is this legislative task that the socialist State will have to accomplish. Between the time when the class-conscious majority of the proletariat, the socialist party, shall take possession of the State in order to give practical effect to its programme, to realize the suppression of classes, and the time when that suppression shall be actually accomplished, there will be an intervening period which will be the socialist phase of the State. During this period, the State will be as always government by a class, but it will be government by that class by which classes, henceforth useless and detrimental, will be suppressed.

In the hands of the socialist party or – what is the same thing – of the organized proletariat, the State will have to regulate the situation of persons and material wealth on the basis of the socialization of capitalist property, and it will control and adjust this situation through the instrumentality of the law. It will act just as the State acted in the last century[28] in the case of the property of the nobility and the clergy, just as the present State acts. It is a tradition of the Revolution that what a law has done a law can undo, and that there is no possible appeal from the decision of the legislative body.

When the socialization of capitalist properly shall have been effected, and legally effected, there will no longer be any economic subordination of some to others, there will be no more classes, and the State, made a necessity by the existence of classes, can at last be suppressed or, rather, it will disappear of itself when it shall have accomplished its task of transformation.

This is not equivalent to saying that the socialist society will have no organization. But the future social organization, when antagonistic classes no longer exist, when constraint no longer has to be exercised over some for the benefit of others, will not be a State any more than the means of production will be capital after they shall have lost the power of exploiting the labor of others, or than the future remuneration will be what we call wages when it shall no longer presuppose surplus-labor. These two latter changes will be the result of the suppression of the character of capital which is to-day stamped upon the principal means of production.

It is needless for me to talk of the future organization, and I limit myself to pointing out the general lines along which it will develop. In the transition period in which the transformation will be accomplished through conscious adaptation of measures to facts, there will still be a State, but that State will be a socialist State. In the following period, the political rule of the men who constituted the State in the transition period, will have become a business administration of affairs, Instead of government there will then be simply a business administration.

Freemen and equals, the producers will decide in common everything concerning production, and henceforth, instead of being the puppets of economic forces beyond their control, they will rule these forces in accordance with their good pleasure. Far from being compelled to submit to a social organization which makes and modifies their conditions of existence without any regard to their wishes, as is the case at present, they will have, for the first time, the kind of social organization which they shall wish – a wish guided by knowledge of the causes and effects of social phenomena. Men will at last be their own masters, The unconscious development of humanity will be followed by a conscious development. Progress, instead of being as before a frequent source of sufferings, will be the source of universal prosperity. Inventions and discoveries – the parents of material prosperity – when introduced into actual practice, will no longer be perverted by social institutions and forced to have effects wholly different from those justly foreseen, intended and expected. The universalization of material comfort and the general comprehension of the conception of social solidarity which will be brought home to the mind of the individual by the perception of the social foundation of his prosperity, will be the starting-point of an intense and vigorous intellectual and ethical development inspired in the individual as in society by the vision of the good, the welfare, the greatest possible welfare of all, and having as its natural consequence the most untrammelled blossoming of individuality, and the freest possible realization of the aspirations of each individual.

To conclude, I am going to sum up this lecture and the results that, I believe, have been correctly reached.

After defining the State by attributing to it a beginning and an end, I investigated the beginnings of the State; I pointed out to you its genesis and I showed that the establishment of the State was a step forward.

At this point, in order to avoid any misapprehension and to reply at the same time to a question raised in this very place, I explained to you what it was that from our point of view constituted this progress, what were its constituent elements and what its consequences.

Bound up, I have tried to demonstrate, with the division of society into classes, the State is a mode of social organization which can persist only so long as that division shall last, and the goal, to attain which all socialist efforts should be directed, is the conquest of the State, the capture of the public powers.

Discussing the objections brought against this thesis, I was led to explain my views on the general strike and to reject it as a socialist weapon.

Therefore, we must work without ceasing to elect more and more socialists to office, to permeate and saturate the State more and more with socialist ideas, until, in the hands of the socialist party or the class-conscious, organized proletariat, the State with all its powers, and especially that of law-making, becomes the instrument, which it is destined to be, of the economic transformation to be accomplished. When that transformation is completely accomplished, there will then be, instead of persons to be constrained, only things to be administered, and on that glorious day there will still be a social organization, but it will no longer be a State.

Footnotes:

1. Published by Chailley, Paris, 1894, p.19.

2. *La Politique*, p. 15.

3. *Idem*, p. 29.

4. *Idem*, p. 29.

5. *Idem*, p. 27.

6. "In primitive society, a body of blood-kindred, descended from a common ancestor, having a common gentile name, and distinguished by a totem or crest." – *Standard Dictionary*.

7. *L'origine de la famille, de la propriété privée et de l'Etat.* – Engels (translated by H. Ravé).

8. *La Politique*, p. 29.

9. *Idem*, p. 29,

10. First Vol. of *Capital*, preface, p. xi., Humboldt Edition.

11. *De l'amour*, chap. liv.

12. "Idealism and Materialism in the Conception of History," a lecture by Jean Jaurès, with a reply by Paul Lafargue. Paris, 1895, pp. 11, 12.

13. "All history is nothing but a continuous transformation of human nature." – Marx,

Misère de la philosophie, p.144.

14. "Man makes his own history, but he does not make it out of the whole cloth; he does not make it out of conditions chosen by himself, but out of such as he finds close at hand. The tradition of all past generations weighs like an Alp upon the brain of the living." – Marx, *The Eighteenth Brumaire of Louis Bonaparte*. International Pub. Co., p. 5.

15. *Misère de la philosophie*, p.114.

16. *La Politique*, p. 25.

17. *Idem.*, pp. 26, 27.

18. *Idem.*, p. 57.

19. *Idem.*, p. 58.

20. *Socialism, Revolution and Internationalism*. International Library Publishing Co.

21. The evils necessarily incident to representative and party government. – Tr.

22. This section is devoted by Deville entirely to the consideration of the "general strike." As I believe the latter has few advocates in America, I have taken the liberty of abridging this section.. – Tr.

23. This French idiom is so expressive, I cannot persuade myself to English it. – Tr.

24. The rest of this section is devoted by Deville to demonstrate with great force the impossibility of the general strike. I omit it for the reason given in the note at the beginning of the section. – Tr.

25. Typifying the attitude of those who look to increasing misery to goad the toilers into socialism. – Tr.

26. Undemocratic, reactionary socialism such as was used as a buffer by Bismarck.

27. *Journal des Débats*, Nov. 1894.

28. This refers to the French Revolution. – Tr .